M000313304

Questions and Answers

for

God Can't

Thomas Jay Oord

SacraSagePress.com

© 2020 SacraSage Press and Thomas Jay Oord

All rights reserved. No part of this book may be reproduced in any form without written consent of the author or SacraSage Press. SacraSage Press provides resources that promote wisdom aligned with sacred perspectives. All rights reserved.

Print: 978-1-948609-31-9

Electronic: 978-1-948609-26-5

Audiobook: 978-1-948609-21-0

Printed in the United States of America

Library of Congress Cataloguing-in-Publication Data

Questions and Answers for God Can't / Thomas Jay Oord

For my students...
past, present, and future
online, in person, and through media
doctoral, masters, undergraduate,
those I know and those I'll never meet

Table of Contents

Preface

I wrote this book to offer answers.

God Can't readers sent me great questions after finishing the book. Most found the book's arguments persuasive. Some readers said the ideas transformed their lives.[1]

For many readers, the book raised additional questions about God, the world, and their personal beliefs. Some questions were theological in orientation. Some were practical and others personal. Nearly every question seemed to have emerged from careful deliberation about the implications of God's uncontrolling love.

Answering each question well would require full-length books. I don't have time to write that many books and you don't have time to read them. I'm providing chapter-length responses here. I apologize for not answering *every* good question I am asked. Drop me an email or a note on social media if you want to ask something I did not address here.

My tone in this book is conversational. At times, my answers may sound academic, but I try to avoid technical language. I intend to be accessible and understandable. I use a tone typical of a podcast interview or popular lecture.

I hope this book becomes a valuable resource in your ongoing quest to love God, others, all creation, and yourself. As I see it, love isn't limited to matters of the heart. It involves the most profound elements of our intellect. In the quest for wisdom, love integrates reason with the widest array of experiences. Answering our questions well can help us love with confidence.

I'm interested to see the response to this book. I don't pretend it offers the last word on every subject. There will always be more to ponder. I don't expect everyone who embraces the uncontrolling love perspective to agree with what I say in this book. But I think these ideas can help you and me explore the implications and applications of God's uncontrolling love.

Thomas Jay Oord

God Can't is Helping People

I wasn't prepared for the impact of **God Can't: How to Believe in God and Love after Tragedy, Abuse, and Other Evils.** Reader responses blew me away!

Several friends urged me to take the idea of God's uncontrolling love and make it accessible to a wider audience. They believed many more would find this view of God fruitful. I was willing to act on their encouragement, because I wanted to expand and add new ideas. *God Can't* was born.

I'm happy to say the book has been an Amazon best-seller in multiple categories. I'm even happier that the ideas in it are helping people. Readers frequently send notes thanking me for introducing them to the uncontrolling love of God perspective. For some, the ideas have been life changing! Others write to say the book helped them connect intellectual dots previously disconnected.

Given the response, it seemed appropriate to begin this book with a brief look at the readers of *God Can't*.

READERS OF *GOD CAN'T*

Most responses to *God Can't* come through email or social media. A few are hand-written and given in person or sent through postal service. Some take me out for coffee to pose questions. And scholars query me, seeking clarity as they explore this fresh perspective.

I want to share a few responses. I've focused on those that offer a taste of the impact *God Can't* is having. All names have been changed to protect the authors.

One of the first notes addressed God and sexual abuse. The writer found helpful the idea God can't stop evil singlehandedly. It would be the first of *many* similar notes...

Let me tell you a bit about my story. I'm a survivor of sexual abuse, a lot and for a long time by my brother. In the midst of the worst years of my life, I had a very vivid dream of God walking over to my bed as I was being raped. God simply reached out, held my hand, and cried.

For a few short days, I was elated: God hadn't left me after all! Then came the anger. Anger that God was there, and instead of stopping it, God simply held my hand and watched!

For a long time, years, I was angry about that. I prayed for a breakthrough. But I never got it, so I buried it. Now paging, praying, and contemplating through your book, I can see more clearly what may have been happening. God could not stop my brother; God gives free will. How could God have stopped him?

The reality is God couldn't, not that God didn't. For me, this is a complete game-changer.

—Monica

Another note addressed how *God Can't* helped the reader think about divine action and childhood cancer. This man told me about his son...

My three-year-old son died from a particularly difficult form of childhood cancer. I can no longer believe the notion that "God is in control." What loving parent would choose to stand by while their child walked into traffic... if that parent could stop the child? I know of none.

When it comes to God, there has to be more than God choosing to allow evil to happen.

—Geoffrey

Many notes addressed the importance of saying God *can't* rather than God *won't*. So many survivors have been told God sometimes chooses to allow evil, which leaves them with painful question. Here's one of those notes...

I've always heard people speak of allowing something. But it never sits well with my soul. If God allows one thing, where do we stop with how much He does allow good or bad? If God can control, where do we stop with that idea?

I've never been able to accept God controls or even allows, because that would mean God allowed my childhood torture. God did not exercise control to stop it. Unacceptable!

This bad view of God has led me to drift in and out of a crisis of faith. I thought God was controlling or allowing the harm I endured. I had no other way to conceptualize it. And I was told it's not okay to ask hard questions.

The idea God can't stop evil singlehandedly articulates what I had intuited but had not yet expressed.

—Cami

A pastor sent a note saying *God Can't* helped him think differently about suffering. The note mirrored several sent by caregivers and spiritual counselors...

As a pastor, I've heard people offer a myriad of ways to make sense of tragedy. Many attribute tragedy to the will of God. They focus on the mystery of God's ways as their way of managing more troubling thoughts about God's choice to harm or allow harm.

While I would not presume to tell a survivor how to make peace with God, many would benefit from the opportunity to consider the "God Can't" option. In it, God neither sent them harm nor stood by and allowed it to take place when God could have done otherwise.

—Jim

A young woman sent me this letter after an event at which I spoke. It represents many letters from survivors and victims who found *God Can't* helpful...

If God could, why would God allow two teenage boys to tie me up to a tree at age eight to be tortured and molested? Then I was told I was defiled, and God couldn't love me anymore.

Why would this God allow that same child to endure an attempted abduction at age 12? Then allow her to be stalked and raped by a man in her church?

I just can't see a God who allows children to go through all of this. I can't see God allowing a woman to be taken into sex slavery, for instance, or allow children to die from horrific diseases.

After reading just part of your book, I can see the God who "allows" these things is not a God of total love.

—Angie

Finally, another note from a pastor:

I finished your book last night, and I just can't stop thinking about it. Thank you for this amazing book! It's a mind-blowing, game-changing book about God's uncontrolling love.

As a cancer survivor and someone who struggles with chemo-induced pulmonary fibrosis, I've tried to make sense of why God allows illnesses. I've struggled with why God heals some people and doesn't heal others. Or why God allows evil and abuse. And so on.

This book provides the first explanation that I've resonated with. I highly recommend it to those who have faced tragedy, abuse, and other evils!

—Pablo

These excerpts are just the tip of the iceberg. *God Can't* is making a powerful impact. As I write this follow-up book, it's been about a year since *God Can't* was published. I fully expect the ideas to help many more people![1]

SUMMING UP

To set the stage for this book, *Questions and Answers for God Can't*, let me briefly review key ideas in *God Can't*. This review will help me as I answer questions in the upcoming chapters.

Let me recap.

God Can't uses true stories to explain why we need a view of God different from what most of us have learned. The book rejects the typical answers to why a good, loving, and powerful God would not prevent evil.

The problem of evil is the primary reason most atheists say they can't believe in God. And I suspect God's relation to evil and suffering is the number one question asked by those who do believe in God.

I often say in *God Can't* that God loves everyone and everything. I define "love" as acting intentionally, in relational response to God and others, to promote overall well-being. This definition applies to the love both creatures and God express. Those who imagine they've solved the problem of evil by saying God's love is entirely different from ours haven't solved the problem at all. Such love is utterly incomprehensible, and such absolute mysteries don't bring us closer to making sense of life.

I also believe genuinely evil events occur. A genuinely evil occurrence makes the world, all things considered, worse than it might have been. Evil events do not make our lives better overall.

Some people reject the idea of evil. But we all act as if we think genuine evils occur. We all act as if some things make the world worse than it might have been. Besides, it's hard to look at horrific events and say they're not genuinely evil. The Christian tradition assumes some events make the world worse, and it calls at least some of them sinful.

God Can't Prevent Evil

The first and probably most controversial point of the book comes in Chapter One: *God can't singlehandedly prevent evil.* It's important to distinguish between saying God *can't* prevent evil and God *won't* prevent evil. Many people will say God won't always prevent evil. They're uncomfortable saying God can't singlehandedly stop it.

A loving person prevents the evil that person is capable of preventing. To think a loving God stands by and allows genuine evil runs counter to what love is really like. It runs counter to the love Jesus expressed. Saying "love allows evil" makes no sense.

I'm not the first theologian to say God can't do some things. The majority say God can't do what is illogical. God can't make 2 + 2 = 387. God can't make a married bachelor. And so on.

Many theologians also say God cannot contradict God's own nature. If it's God's nature to exist, God must exist. If it's God's nature to love, God must love. God simply can't act in an evil way or cease to exist.

Biblical writers sometimes mention actions God cannot take. My favorite example comes from the Apostle Paul's letter to Timothy. "When we are faithless," writes Paul, "God remains faithful, because God *cannot* deny himself" (2 Tim. 2:13).

My purpose in saying that God must do some things and can't do others says God's love is inherently uncontrolling.

Divine love is self-giving and others-empowering. Because God necessarily loves everyone and everything, God must self-give and others-empower. This means God can't control anyone or anything. Uncontrolling love comes first in God's nature.

Saying God can't make round squares, can't stop existing, or can't control others leads us to wonder if God is limited. The uncontrolling love view seems to describe a God with limited powers, at least compared to how most people think of God.

Most people have an incoherent view of God. They say or think God can do things inherently impossible for loving beings to do. Incoherent theology does not appeal to thinking people.

In chapter one, I also explore an idea most Christians, Jews, and Muslims affirm: that God does not have a localized body like we do. Instead, God is an omnipresent bodiless spirit. God is incorporeal, to use the classic language.

Saying God is bodiless helps us understand why we sometimes can use our bodies to thwart evil, but God can't thwart them. We can sometimes grab someone from falling into a pit, for instance. But God doesn't have a divine hand to grab falling people.

All good ultimately stems from God, because God is the source of good. When we use our arms to rescue people from pits, we can say God inspired our bodily actions. We act as God's metaphorical hands and feet. This doesn't mean we're literally gods or literally divine. But when we respond to the Spirit and do something loving, we can believe God was the inspirational source of our actions.

I also briefly address the role of mystery in the first chapter of *God Can't*. Many believers play the mystery card when the questions of God and evil emerge. "God's ways are not our ways," they say. Or "We don't understand why a loving God doesn't stop evil."

I don't play this mystery card, meaning I don't appeal to mystery rather than rethinking my view of God. I don't think I know God completely. And what I think I know about God, I don't know with absolute certainty. In that sense, even I have a role for mystery. But that role is different from playing the mystery card instead of rethinking our fundamental ideas about God. That's an idea we'll return to in future chapters.

Some who see the title, *God Can't* wonder if I'll be describing a God who watches from a distance. Or a God who does nothing at all. But the God I describe is active throughout all existence, and we all rely upon God's moment-by-moment activity.

God Feels Our Pain

The second big idea in *God Can't* says that *God feels pain*. God empathizes with those who suffer. "The Golden Rule" says we should do to others, as we would have them do to us. What I call "The Crimson Rule" says we should feel with others, as we would have them feel with us.

God is the fellow sufferer who understands. God is moved with compassion and affected by the ups and downs of our lives. God empathizes with us better than any friend could. We see this empathy most clearly in the person of Jesus of Nazareth.

Most Christian theologians have said God does not suffer. Most say God is impassable or non-relational. But the God I see described in Scripture, in Jesus, and active in the world not only influences us but is also influenced by us. God engages in giving and receiving relationships.

To solve the problem of evil, it's not enough to say God suffers with us. Some contemporary theologians affirm the idea God empathizes, but they offer, "God suffers with us" as their only answer to the problem of evil.

It's important to believe God suffers with us, but we should also believe God can't prevent evil singlehandedly. Without both ideas (and others in *God Can't*), we can't offer a believable explanation for unnecessary suffering, tragedy, abuse, and other evils.

I close Chapter Two of *God Can't* by listing ways we might feel God's love. I mention six such ways. One involves the ministry of human presence. For this, I recommend therapy and counseling. The second way is through communities of care. I readily acknowledge some faith communities don't love and care, so I recommend searching for those that do. The third way we might feel God's love is through practices like meditation, mindfulness, and prayer. Some of these activities are classic and well known; others may be new to you. Fourth, we sometimes feel God's presence in nature. I often hike in parts of the world that inspire me. The fifth way we sometimes experience God's love is through art, music, and movies. Finally, the sixth is our love for or from children, a powerful means to feel God's loving presence.

God Works to Heal

The third big idea in *God Can't* offers a framework of ideas to understand healing. God works to heal, but healing does not always occur. To reconstruct our views of healing, I offer four general beliefs.

First, *God is always present to all aspects of creation*. God never intervenes, as if coming from the outside. As one present to all creation, God always works to heal to the greatest extent possible, given the circumstances. God is the source for *all* healing that occurs.

Second, *God works alongside people, their bodies, aspects of creation, and other entities.* God works with healthcare professionals, nurses, pharmacists, medical specialists, nutritionists, and so on. God works alongside people with unique healing gifts, communities of faith, and commonsense folk wise in the ways of living. God also works alongside cells, organs, blood, muscles, and other body entities.

Third, although God always works to heal, *God can't heal singlehandedly.* God's healing work is always uncontrolling, because God always loves and never controls. Creation must cooperate. This does not mean those not healed did not have enough faith. People often have plenty of cooperative faith and work with the Great Physician. But their bodies or other factors are not conducive to God's healing work. Circumstances in our bodies and beyond them present both opportunities and challenges. Because God can't overpower or bypass agents and entities, God can't singlehandedly heal. Healing comes when creatures or entities cooperate or when the inanimate conditions of creation are conducive to healing.

Fourth, *some healing must wait until the afterlife.* I believe in continued subjective experience beyond bodily death. While there is much speculation in Scripture and among serious thinkers about what happens in the afterlife, I argue that our personal experience continues without our present bodies.

God Squeezes Good from Bad

The fourth big idea says we don't have to think God wants evil for good to emerge. We can believe God always works for good despite pain, torture, and traumas. God works with us, our bodies, smaller entities, and the larger society to squeeze whatever good can be squeezed from the bad God didn't want in the first place.

We don't have to believe everything happens for a reason. We don't have to believe God allows suffering to improve our character. We don't have to think God sends pain to punish us or teach us a lesson. Instead, we should believe God works to wring a measure of wellness from the wrong God didn't want.

God is not an outside force predetermining the course of our lives. God moves through time with us and the future is yet to be decided. When rotten things happen, God doesn't give up on the situation. God works with us and other agents, possibilities, circumstances, and data to bring whatever good can be brought from bad.

God doesn't punish. But there are natural negative consequences that come from sin and evil. Sometimes those who experience negative consequences are not the ones who failed to love. In an interrelated universe, the harmful actions of one can hurt others more than the harming actor. Evildoers and the unrighteous sometimes seem to be better off, at least in the short term.

When our suffering produces character, helps us learn a lesson, or provides wisdom, we don't have to believe God caused or allowed it to bring about good. Instead, we can say God worked to squeeze something good out of the evil God didn't want in the first place.

God Needs Our Cooperation

The final idea in *God Can't* says God needs cooperation for love to win. Instead of believing God can singlehandedly establish the ways of love, we should believe in what I call "indispensable love synergy." This synergy says God calls and empowers our responses of love.

Conventional theologians say God doesn't need us. The conventional God is like the preschool teacher who tells her kids to clean up a playroom and says they won't go home unless the room is clean. But when the children don't cooperate, she does the job herself. Traditional theologies portray God as condescending to ask us to participate in what God can do without our help. They imply our lives don't ultimately matter.

By contrast, the God of uncontrolling love needs us. Our choices, our lives, our decisions are ultimately important. God does not need us for God to exist; God will exist no matter what happens. God's needs are the needs of love. If love is relational and the results for which love aims rely upon our responses, God's needs are based on love.

We need not fear the God of uncontrolling love. God never harms us or others. We should work with God to protect ourselves and others, as God calls us to protect the weak, vulnerable, and defenseless.

Near the end of chapter five, I offer what I call the "relentless love" view of the afterlife. It says that God never gives up inviting us to relationship in this life and the next. We can always say no to love. But God never gives up inviting us to abundant life. I'll spend an entire chapter in the present book exploring the afterlife in more detail.

In sum, the five key ideas of *God Can't* provide an actual solution for why a loving and powerful God does not prevent genuine evil. These ideas, taken together, present a loving God whom we can trust without reservation.

GOD'S NATURE OF LOVE

Many readers of *God Can't* ask questions that directly or indirectly deal with my view of God's uncontrolling love. In my more academic book, *The Uncontrolling Love of God: An Open and Relational Account of Providence*, I call this view "essential kenosis." It wrestles with how we might best understand God's nature of love.[2]

Even some professional theologians avoid speculating about God's nature. Some say we should only talk about how God acts in the world. But I think it's natural to wonder who God is when we see actions we think are God-inspired.

The Bible can help us ponder God's nature. The revelation of God we find in Jesus is particularly illuminating. When we speculate about God's nature, we draw wisdom from the Christian tradition, contemporary experiences, sages and saints, science, the humanities, our own reasoning abilities, and more.

Our vision of God's nature will always be partly obscured and ambiguous. And we should be humble and tentative. But we have good reasons to believe we can make progress in understanding God, even if we can't be certain.

I believe love comes logically first in God's nature. By "first," I don't mean God's attributes line up like dominoes, and love is the first in line. I mean we should think about God's other attributes in light of love. Love should come first conceptually as we think about God.

God has other attributes, and they're important. But when our views of those attributes clash with love, we need to reformulate them in ways that harmonize with love.

When some hear me place conceptual priority on love, they'll say, "Why not make God's attributes equal, so none has priority?" Some theologians have tried to do this. But if we examine their theologies, we find they (at least implicitly) privilege some divine attributes over others.

For instance, some theologians say God's love and power are equal. But then they'll claim God has the power not to love. Or they'll say God could decide to stop loving someone. These claims reveal such theologians actually think God's power of choice comes logically prior to love. By contrast, I think love comes logically before power.

I'm not the first theologian to say love comes first in God's nature, although this view is in the minority. Nor am I the first to say God must love, although this strikes many people as unusual. I don't know anyone else, however, who adds the particular content I do when saying love comes first in God's nature. It's this content I call "essential kenosis" or "uncontrolling love" theology.

We interpret the Bible well when we use essential kenosis as our interpretive lens. This view says God cannot override, withdraw, or fail to provide the power of freedom, agency, or existence to creaturely others. Consequently, God can't control creatures or creation.

Most kenosis theologians think God voluntarily chooses to self-give power and freedom to creation. Most say God self-limits voluntarily and decides to allow space for creatures to act freely. Jürgen Moltmann is a good representative of this view of divine kenosis as voluntarily self-limiting. But the God who voluntarily self-limits could choose to un-self-limit at any time. In theologies like Moltmann's, sovereign choice to self-limit comes first in God's nature.[3] So victims and survivors wonder why God didn't un-self-limit to rescue them singlehandedly!

By contrast, essential kenosis says God is involuntarily self-limited.[4] God is self-limited in the sense that no outside force, power, or authority limits God. God's loving nature limits God's action. Consequently, God can't control others. The God who cannot control others cannot prevent evil singlehandedly.

JOHN WESLEY SAYS GOD CAN'T

I conclude this chapter by looking briefly at words from John Wesley, one of my theological heroes. It surprises even some Wesleyan scholars that Wesley claimed God could not do some things. In his sermon "On Providence," he wrestles with how to say God acts. He writes:

> *"Were human liberty taken away, men would be as incapable of virtue as stones. Therefore (with reverence be it spoken), the Almighty himself cannot do this thing. God cannot thus contradict himself or undo what he has done."*

Notice Wesley says God *cannot* do these things. He doesn't say God *chooses* not to do them. Some activities are simply not possible for an almighty God.

Wesley makes three claims in this quote. First, he says (as I do) God can't take away freedom. Secondly, he says (as I do) God can't contradict himself. And third, Wesley claims (as I do) God can't undo what has been done.

Many Christian theologians accept that God can't take away freedom. They may say God can't undermine the freedom God gives. I make the stronger argument that God *must* give freedom to complex creatures, because God's loving nature requires it. And I argue God necessarily gives agency and self-organization to smaller creatures and entities. These gifts of love are why God can't withdraw, override, or fail to give freedom, agency, or self-organization to creatures and creation.[5]

The second idea in Wesley's quote says God can't contradict God's own nature. This fits nicely with my essential kenosis theology. We might say God can't decide not to be God. This idea is central to Christian theologians who say God's essence comes prior to God's will. We'll look at this more in later chapters.

The third idea in Wesley's quote refers to God's inability to change what has already occurred. What's done is done; reverse causation is a myth. God works to *redeem* the past, but that's not the same as changing it. Wesley seems to make a claim about God's relation to time. Although he was not an open theist in the contemporary sense of that label, he endorses a view about God's relation to time that open theists like me appreciate. I suspect that if Wesley were living today, he'd identify as open and relational.

I mention John Wesley not to indicate that I'm merely presenting ideas he previously offered. There are similarities. But I'm making some bolder moves than Wesley made. While I'm not the first theologian to say God can't, my contributions explain how a particular view of God's nature resolves the problem of evil.

CONCLUSION

In this book, I'm widening the conversation. I will show how the uncontrolling love view resolves perplexing questions and concerns. Readers will probably be surprised at how my answers are both radical and yet compatible with beliefs held by every-day people.

The advantages of saying God can't do some activities because divine love is uncontrolling are wide ranging. I've addressed some in *God Can't* and *The Uncontrolling Love of God*. Other writers explore the view's benefits in a book called *Uncontrolling Love: Essays Exploring the Love of God with Introductions by Thomas Jay Oord.*[6]

Many questions remain unanswered... or at least not answered as sufficiently as they could be. So... let's get to those questions. That's the purpose of this book!

I begin each chapter with a question that, in some form, has been posed to me. Some questions come from the Facebook group "The Uncontrolling Love of God Conversations" and other online discussion groups. Some come from lectures, as I've traveled across the U.S. and Europe. Some come from emails, social media, podcast interviews, conversations at coffee shops, and more.

I strive to keep each chapter short. And I try to write as plainly as possible. I hope you'll see how the uncontrolling love of God perspective you encountered in *God Can't* answers many other important questions!

CHAPTER ONE

If God can't control, why pray?

I often hear this chapter's question. Readers of *God Can't* ask it in emails. I hear it from live audiences and podcast hosts. Many wonder what implications the uncontrolling love view has for prayer.

I appreciate this question. It shows that readers take seriously these theological ideas and want to explore their consequences. Many readers want to integrate *God Can't* ideas into their devotional lives and ways of living.

Prayer takes many forms, of course. The question framing this chapter falls under what many call "petitionary prayer." This involves asking God to do something. If God can't single-handedly control others to fix some problem or grant some wish, we might wonder why we should ask.

I spend most of this chapter exploring petitionary prayer. But near the end, I talk about what it means to pray in thanks, praise, and worship. The uncontrolling love of God view has positive implications for these forms of prayer too.

A CONTROLLING GOD AND A CORONAVIRUS VICTIM

Before answering this chapter's question, let me look at two alternative views of God and prayer. Each has negative implications for understanding petitionary prayer believers seldom realize.

To help us see what these alternative views of prayer entail, let's take the hypothetical case of Tim. As I write this book, Coronavirus/COVID-19 is killing hundreds of thousands of people and causing widespread harm. Let's suppose Tim has contracted the virus and wants us to pray for his health.

What prayers make sense?

Some people believe God controls absolutely everything. This is the "All God" view I mentioned in *God Can't*. It claims God does everything, because God is the omnicause. "God is sovereignly in control," say people who embrace this view.

The All God view rejects the idea we're genuinely free. God predetermines every moment of every creature. Most All God advocates believe God predestined all things from the foundation of the universe. And the God who predestines can foreknow everything that will happen.

So... if a person believes God controls everything, what does this mean we should say when praying for Tim?

The All God view says God caused the Coronavirus. It's God's will. Most who affirm this view believe God predestined the Coronavirus to kill, wreak havoc in the world, and sicken millions. Before the foundation of the world, God decided the virus would sicken Tim in particular. It's all part of God's meticulous blueprint.

If I believed the All God view, I could not bring myself to petition God. I would not pray for Tim. Here's why...

Petitionary prayer involves asking God to do something in the future. But the God who predetermined everything can't respond to such prayers. The future is already settled, and what will occur has already decided. If God predetermined Tim to contract the virus, my prayers make no difference to helping him. Asking God to do something new makes no sense.

In fact, my request for Tim's healing seems to oppose God's will. From the All God perspective, after all, God wanted Tim to be sick. And acting against God's will is, by definition, sin. Praying for Tim would be sinning!

I can't get inspired to ask something of a God for whom my actions make no difference. Besides, if the All God view is true that God wills everything, God wills that I can't get inspired to pray for Tim!

THE CONVENTIONAL GOD AND CORONAVIRUS VICTIM

Most people I know don't believe the All God view. Most believe they act freely, at least sometimes. Most think the future has not been predestined, even if they say God (mysteriously) knows everything that will occur. This leads to our second view of God and prayer.

The second view assumes what I call the "Conventional" view of God. People who believe in the Conventional view think God singlehandedly fixes things from time to time. But they think God usually allows the free processes of existence and free creatures to exert influence too.

Many people who identify as "classical Arminians" embrace this view of prayer. It says God can and sometimes does singlehandedly bring about results, cure people, stop evil, and so on. God foreknows everything that will ever occur without determining all of it. This God doesn't control everything but sometimes controls some things.

So, does this view make sense when praying for Tim?

Not really. The Conventional God is allegedly perfectly loving, has controlling power, and knows in advance everything that will ever occur. This God could heal Tim without our prayers, cooperation, medicine, or creaturely influences. And yet... this God rarely heals. Tim suffers from a virus the Conventional God foreknew and could stop singlehandedly but has refused to do so.

Conventional theology implies God sometimes requires prayer to get him off his butt and do what's loving. Believers must beg, plead, or twist God's arm to get good results. But if Tim is not healed, he'll wonder if God has abandoned him, is punishing him, or this allows evil to teach a lesson. It's confusing.

If God loves everyone and everything and can singlehandedly fix anything, why do we need to ask for help? Wouldn't this God automatically fix what is fixable? And if God foreknows with certainty what will occur, petitionary prayer cannot change an already foreknown and therefore settled future.

MY DAUGHTER IS DROWNING

To explain why petitionary prayer makes little sense if the Conventional view is true, let me give an illustration.

Suppose I'm out with my family at a lake, and we're enjoying a scorching summer afternoon. I look up from reading and see one of my daughters in the lake. In just a few seconds, I realize my daughter is drowning! Her head is bobbing up and down, and her arms are flailing. She's gasping for air!

Suppose I could jump in and rescue my daughter. I'm a decent swimmer, and it's likely I could save her life. But suppose I say, "She hasn't asked for help. She's not crying out, 'Help me, Dad.' So, I won't rescue her until she asks." Or suppose I say, "I'm not seeing anyone else begging me to save her. Unless 10 people ask, I will not leave the beach!"

No one would think I was a loving father if I could have rescued my drowning daughter but refused because I didn't hear her ask. No one would say, "She didn't ask for help, so he didn't help. That was the loving thing to do." Nor would anyone think I was loving if I waited for 10 people to ask me to help.

The Conventional view portrays God as having the ability to rescue singlehandedly but not always doing so unless we ask. It portrays God as metaphorically sitting back, arms folded, waiting for us to pray, or pray enough, before jumping in to help. Or it portrays God as waiting until a prayer chain of enough people intercede.

The Conventional God could singlehandedly heal Tim, prevent his illness, and fix just about anything. But for some mysterious reason, this God sometimes needs to be asked.

The Conventional view can't portray God as consistently loving. The God who could singlehandedly prevent evil but waits for us to ask is not a God of perfect love. A loving God who can save singlehandedly wouldn't require us to beg, plead, or petition 352 times before healing Tim.

PETITIONARY PRAYER AND THE UNCONTROLLING GOD
Petitionary prayer makes more sense in the uncontrolling love perspective. It assumes a relational view: God gives and receives in a relational world with relational creatures.

To many people, it's obviously true that creation influences God. That's the general view of God portrayed in the Bible, and it fits what many believers think today. The God who is angry at sin or blessed by praise is One whom creatures affect.

It surprises many to discover theologians of yesteryear disagreed. These thinkers believed God was unaffected by what happens in our lives and in the world. They said God was "impassible," to use the classic language. This means God is not compassionate in the way we understand compassion. It also means our prayers make no difference to God, because according to this view, God is not relational.

The uncontrolling love perspective fits the way most people pray, because most believe their prayers may affect God. God not only affects us and influences all creation moment by moment, we and all creation affect God. From the uncontrolling love view, petitionary prayer affects God. This is the first point for understanding prayer in a *God Can't* perspective.

The idea creatures are relational is the second important aspect for understanding petitionary prayer from a *God Can't* perspective. Creation is interconnected; action in one place affects those in others. My actions affect you; your actions affect me. Those actions may primarily be physical or mainly mental. But everything we do — including our prayers — affects ourselves and the world.

In the past, I would need to illustrate the idea creation is interconnected. But nearly everyone acknowledges this reality today. Our decisions affect our bodies, friends and family, societies, and the environment. Praying is an activity.

When we combine the idea that prayer affects God with the idea prayer affects ourselves and others, we can see how prayer makes a difference to an uncontrolling God and to the world. Added to this is the truth that life moves on moment by moment. The past is complete, the present is becoming what it will be, and the future is open. God relates with us moment by moment as the Living Lover of history.[1] Our prayer in one moment influences what is possible in the next. And the God who is present to all receives our actions each moment. This means our prayers open up new avenues for God to work. Fresh opportunities emerge each moment because we prayed. Prayer generates new relationships, data, forces, factors, and information for God to respond to when deciding how to act in the next moment. Because we pray, God may have alternative paths to operate in, new cooperative agents to work with, and new opportunities to influence us and others.

Prayer changes history.

When I say prayer influences God and the world, I'm **not** saying prayer controls others or creation. I'm **not** saying our prayers guarantee the results we want. And I'm **not** saying prayer allows God to control. Petitionary prayer doesn't "turbocharge" God to determine results singlehandedly. Our prayers are not coins in a vending machine that automatically dispenses the drink we want.

Prayer makes a difference, but it doesn't control.

This point is so important that I want to emphasize it. An uncontrolling love view says petitionary prayer makes a difference without fully determining others. It says our prayers affect God without saying prayers make it possible for God to determine others fully. It says praying opens new possibilities God can use in the next moment, without saying those possibilities *guarantee* the rescuing, healing, or blessing we seek. Prayer can be a factor in the good that occurs, but it doesn't guarantee it.

In one sense, the uncontrolling love view fits what most believers think about God's response to their prayers. Most doubt, for instance, their prayers *force* God to control. Few pray, "Dear God, *force* Uncle Joe to become loving." Few pray, "God, control Jennifer to *make* her become a Christian." Most people think God is uncontrollable, so our prayers don't force God to do anything. I agree.

I think God is both uncontrollable and uncontrolling. We can't control God, and there's no sense trying. God is uncontrollable. But God can't control us, others, or anything in creation. God is uncontrolling. God loves everyone and everything, so God can't control anyone or anything.

"Controlling love" is an oxymoron.

PRAYING WITH TIM

Let's return to Tim, the Coronavirus victim. I want to spell out concretely what petitionary prayer might look like in his case.

Let's imagine Tim hospitalized by Coronavirus symptoms, and I've been asked to pray with him. What should I say? How might I pray in a way that makes sense if I believe God can't control?

Acknowledge Suffering

After taking the necessary precautions, I approach Tim to pray. Typically, my first thought is to vocalize the problem. I acknowledge Tim's suffering. I might say,

Loving God, we are in this hospital because Tim is suffering. You know the pain and struggle he endures, and we know it too. This virus is wracking Tim's body and affecting him negatively in so many ways.

Before moving to the second part of my prayer, let me analyze the first. Acknowledging Tim's suffering doesn't inform God that Tim is sick, as if God was previously unaware. God knows the situation better than Tim and I do, in fact, even better than physicians and nurses. God isn't clueless.

Acknowledging this suffering aloud is doing something new, however. Tim is presumably listening. Often part of the healing process is knowing others empathize with us, see us, hear us, or have some understanding of what we endure. Something powerful can occur when sufferers know others perceive their pain and suffer with them.

In addition, Tim's mind influences his body. Humans have a psychosomatic unity, which means the mental affects the physical, and the physical affects the mental. My words of acknowledgement and empathy not only influence Tim's thought patterns, they influence his ill body. My words and their influence provide God extra causal factors God might use in future work with Tim. My prayer, in other words, is already making a difference.

Acknowledge God's Work to Heal

The second aspect of my prayer acknowledges God's activity.

We acknowledge your efforts to heal Tim. We believe you are the Great Physician. You are working right now

to the greatest extent possible to bring about healing.
Thank you for your healing activities.

Let's analyze this second aspect. If the uncontrolling love of God view is correct, God always works to heal to the greatest extent possible (for details on this, see chapter three of *God Can't*). My saying, "We acknowledge your efforts to heal" isn't telling God something new about what God has been doing. It's not like God thinks, "Oh, so that's what I've been up to lately. Who knew?!"

Acknowledging God's work to heal does something new at this moment, however. My prayer tells Tim something new or reminds him of something he's known: God wants to heal. God doesn't sit around twiddling thumbs waiting to be asked. God wants to heal everyone and everything, and God always works to heal to the greatest extent possible. Acknowledging God as a healer is important for Tim's mental state. His mental state affects the state of his body. So, my saying God is already working to heal may provide new possibilities and avenues for God in the healing process.

Acknowledge Opposition to Healing

Let's move to the third phase of my prayer.

We know you, God, are facing forces and factors —
specifically, a virus — opposing the healing you want.
We know principalities and powers of various types
sometimes run counter to the good you want in our
lives and in creation.

Let's analyze this third phase. In this, I'm acknowledging aloud God doesn't have the power to erase all opposition by absolute fiat or decree. I'm endorsing the uncontrolling love view and assuming God can't singlehandedly prevent evil.

Tim might interpret "forces, factors, principalities, and powers" as a reference to demonic beings. He might think these words refer to natural causes. I specifically identified the virus, but his interpretation depends largely on his worldview. I probably won't engage Tim on whether demonic agents or natural factors caused the virus.[2] But I want to put in his mind the idea that God works to heal but faces obstacles, opposition, and resistance.

This third aspect of the prayer is crucial. I don't want Tim to think God has the controlling power that many claim. Many believers pray in ways that imply God can singlehandedly fix all problems. People who suffer like Tim, therefore, expect unilateral healing... but are often not healed.

Most of us know firsthand the problems that come with thinking God can singlehandedly heal. We who are ill, injured, abused, or suffering may wonder if God truly loves us. We wonder if God is punishing or has abandoned us. We wonder if, in some mysterious way, our pain and suffering are an unfortunate part of some divine plan. And so on.

It's crucial to believe God cannot singlehandedly overcome opposition to God's healing work.

Commit to Cooperating with God

Let's move to the fourth phase of my prayer for Tim. In this phase, I pray words of commitment:

At this moment, God, we commit ourselves to cooperate with your healing work. Tim does, and so do I. We commit to following what we believe is best in this situation, such as heeding the counsel of physicians, nurses, and health care workers. We want to sleep well and drink fluids. We commit to cooperating with you to fight this illness.

In our analysis of this fourth phase, it should be clear these words are explicit commitments to cooperate with God's healing. We're not just providing new information. We're committing to do our part in the healing work. Commitment to cooperate doesn't guarantee instantaneous healing or even healing at all. But Tim's present promise and future actions have an actual effect on his body and mental state.

I've already mentioned the psychosomatic interaction between Tim's mind and body. In future chapters, I will offer a philosophical framework for making sense of this. Here I simply want to say Tim's mind doesn't control his body. A commitment to cooperate with God's healing doesn't mean Tim's cells, organs, and other bodily members will automatically reject the virus. Commitments to cooperate bring instantaneous healing on only the rarest of occasions. And when they do, it wasn't the person's cooperation alone that cured the illness.

Our minds affect our bodies, and our bodies affect our minds. But no aspect of ourselves controls other aspects. Sometimes our minds cooperate with God fully, and yet our bodies do not. Sometimes external factors cause us harm that neither our bodies nor minds can resist. And sometimes our bodily members cooperate with God when we mentally do not cooperate. We are complex creatures in a complex world.

Asking God for Help

I'm now to the part of the prayer we normally consider petition. At this point, I might say,

*Help us know how we might cooperate with your heal-
ing work. Give us insight. We also ask that you comfort
Tim as much as is possible in this fight for healing. We
seek your guidance.*

These words present requests of God. But the previous aspects of my prayer have also been making a difference to God
and creation. In one sense, all prayer is petitionary, if we understand "petition" as "having an impact upon" God. All of life is
petitionary prayer, in that sense, because *everything* we do influences God's experience. I think about this when pondering
the Apostle Paul's recommendation to "pray without ceasing"
(1 Thess. 5:17).

We usually think of petitionary prayer as a series of specific
requests. The specific requests I'm making for Tim pertain to
what he needs. I'm asking God to give us wisdom and insight
on how to cooperate with God's healing work. And I'm asking
God to comfort Tim. I could add additional petitions, depending on the situation. God responds to all our requests by calling
various agents, factors, and forces to join in God's work.

When petitioning God, I don't assume giving wisdom,
comfort, insight, inspiration, and so on involves God controlling
us and others. I'm not asking God to do activities only possible for a controlling God. God's responses to petitionary prayer
involve creaturely causes. Not only can we humans cooperate

with the Spirit, other creatures and entities can too, given their abilities.

Acknowledge God's Love

I conclude my prayer by thanking God for loving Tim:

Whether in sickness or health, in sorrow or joy, we believe you love Tim. You love all creation. And in love, you work for our good in all things, God. Thanks for your loving kindness and compassion.

Amen.

When I leave the hospital, I want Tim to realize God cares deeply about him. The uncontrolling love of God view of prayer places love first. It says God desires and acts for Tim's well-being and the well-being of all creation. And that involves God's compassionate care.

I also want to leave the hospital knowing I did not give Tim the impression God can singlehandedly cure him. His partnership with God can make a difference, as well as the cooperation of other people, factors, and actors. This collaboration doesn't guarantee healing, because other factors may oppose God's work for Tim's health. But cooperation makes a difference in the work of healing.[3]

THANKSGIVING

I turn now from petition to prayers of gratitude. The *God Can't* view has positive implications for how we think about thanksgiving. If this view is correct, thanking an uncontrolling God makes sense.

Let's take the Thanksgiving holiday meal as a case study for prayers of gratitude.

Each November, Americans gather with family or friends to celebrate the Thanksgiving holiday. Words of thanks sometimes enter the public news or get expressed at civic gatherings. It's natural to wonder what people believe when they say, "Thank you, God."

One group of people doesn't believe in God. Many of them feel thankful, but their Thanksgiving language has no ultimate Referent. In their view, no Divine Being exists to which their gratitude ultimately points. Giving thanks to God may a way to admit they've been recipients of goodness. Although these unbelievers may say, "Thank you, God," their disbelief a Being exists to whom they should be grateful makes their statement confusing.

Those who say God controls everything — the All God people — express gratitude at Thanksgiving. The God they believe in directly or indirectly controls everything. In their Thanksgiving prayer, they can say, "Thank you, God, for ____," and insert any event. Such events might be supremely joyful or utterly horrific. The God who controls everything is responsible for every act of respect and rape, for peace and pain, for havens or holocausts. Most All God prayers focus on the good. Reminding All God advocates that their God causes evil dampens the holiday spirit!

Conventional theology advocates also pray at Thanksgiving. They usually reject the idea God causes evil, but they claim God allows it. When they're giving thanks, they try to sidestep the theological problems that come with saying God allows evil.

They'll blame free agents or natural forces and ignore the question of why a God who can singlehandedly stop evil permits unnecessary suffering. The God who can control others failed to prevent the dastardly deeds we endure.

When people who accept the Conventional view of God pray at Thanksgiving, they *could* insert any event into "Thank you, God, for _____." The God of Conventional theology gets ultimate credit or blame for causing or allowing all things.

Thanksgiving prayers make more sense in the uncontrolling love of God perspective. Advocates of this view thank the God who always gives freedom, agency, or existence to creatures and creation. God presents a spectrum of possibilities to each creature in each moment.

God is the gracious source for all that's good.

The uncontrolling God actively loves, moment by moment, by providing, inspiring, empowering, and interacting with creation. And this God calls all creatures to respond in love. The genuine evil in the world results from the responses creatures make contrary to God's calls, or from the natural accidents and free processes of reality.

In her Thanksgiving prayer, an advocate of the uncontrolling love view can say every good and perfect gift originates in God. An active but uncontrolling God is the source of goodness and blessing but can't singlehandedly prevent evil. The good we enjoy involves creaturely responses to God's gracious action.

The uncontrolling love view supports our urge to thank creatures at Thanksgiving. Most believers thank one another from time to time, as if they intuitively know creatures join with God to do good. It's right to thank God for acting as the ultimate source of goodness, but we should also thank those who cooperate with God. We can thank God and the cook!

The more we realize how interrelated the universe is and how much God loves in an uncontrolling way, the more we understand how widely we are indebted. A Thanksgiving meal is possible because of God's action, a chef or chefs, farmers, those who transport food, those who make the plates, tables, and homes we use when celebrating, and so many more. God inspires goodness throughout all creation.

We have many reasons to be thankful... and many to thank!

PRAYERS OF PRAISE AND WORSHIP

I conclude with a few comments on prayers of praise and worship. These activities have been the center of how believers understand God's activity. Believers express prayers of praise and worship both corporately and individually. A perfectly loving, powerful, and beautiful God is worthy of praise and worship!

Unfortunately, many prayers of worship or songs of praise place priority upon God's power to the detriment of God's love. God is powerful, but I often hear language that frames God's love in light of power rather than the opposite. I could point to examples in "low church" worship choruses and in the "high church" prayers of praise.

Many worship songs stress sovereignty when speaking of God's glory. "God is in control," they proclaim. "God orchestrates every lightning strike and falling leaf." Some songs ask God to "take my will" or say God's ways are "irresistible." Taken literally, many worship songs assume God is or could be controlling.

I can't worship a God who could singlehandedly control but chooses not to prevent evil. By "worship," I mean give whole-hearted trust and devotion. I can't whole-heartedly trust a God who could prevent evil but chooses not to do so. I can't be entirely devoted to an inconsistently loving deity. It's more than an intellectual inability. My inability to worship a controlling God is visceral!

The idea we should praise controlling power is deeply ingrained in most of us. When some hear that I can't worship a controlling God, they respond in shock. Some wonder, "Is a God who *can't* control even worth worshipping?"

I respond to this rhetorical question by saying my worship is unreserved and whole-hearted. I worship without qualms a God who loves everyone and everything but can't control anyone or anything. Without crossing my fingers, I stand in amazement. As I see it, God's glory derives primarily from God's steadfast love.

The question of worship has implications for ethics. A full exploration, like many of these topics, requires a book-length response. But let me say a few words.

What we think God is like affects how we think we ought to live. If we think God is uncontrolling and loves at all times and places, this can motivate us to imitate God by loving in an uncontrolling way at all times and places. If we think God is in control, calls the shots, and is in charge, it's natural to think we ought at least sometimes to be in control, call the shots, and be in charge. Trying to control others leads to ruin, however. An ethics of uncontrolling love says we ought to influence others for good without controlling them.[4]

The uncontrolling love perspective has powerful implications for how we ought to act!

IF GOD CAN'T CONTROL, WHY PRAY?

Prayer comes in many forms. We should engage in petitionary prayer, because it affects God and creation. Our prayers open new possibilities and opportunities for God and others. Prayer neither controls God nor makes God able to control others. We can't control an uncontrollable God, and an uncontrolling God can't control us. But prayer makes an actual difference to the Creator and to creation.

The uncontrolling love of God perspective provides a satisfying overall framework to understand prayer. I'm motivated to pray when I believe God cannot control but lovingly influences all. My inclination to pray in thanks and praise makes sense from a *God Can't* perspective. It makes far less sense if God can or does control others.

As I prayed this morning, I used a breathing exercise. I imagined breathing into my lungs God's loving presence. I inhaled. I then imagined breathing out love for others, God, myself, and all creation. I exhaled. I inhaled God's empowering love and exhaled my response of love. This is a symbolic expression of what I think literally occurs, as God loves moment-by-moment and calls for response.

I hope this view of an uncontrolling God influenced by our petitions inspires you to pray.

CHAPTER TWO

If God is uncontrolling, how do we explain miracles?

To answer this chapter's question, let me share some inside information about how my book The Uncontrolling Love of God *took shape.*

This academic book explores models of God's action in the world. This research usually falls under the category "divine providence." When I originally proposed the book idea to my editor, David Congdon, I said I'd write seven chapters. While writing the final chapter, I realized I had not addressed miracles. I emailed David and said I needed to add an eighth chapter.

I realized many conservative and progressive readers would wonder how I understood miracles in light of God's uncontrolling love. My beliefs about miracles had undergone change, but I'd done no academic research on the subject. As I wrote the chapter, I had questions of my own.

WHAT IS A MIRACLE?

My research unearthed few definitions of miracles. Well, few *good* definitions. A tiny number of theologians, Bible scholars, philosophers, or scientists offer any definition, and few made sense to me.

In philosophical discussions, David Hume's ideas on miracles are central. This eighteenth-century Scottish philosopher understood a miracle to be an event that violates the laws of nature or interrupts the causal patterns of existence. According to Hume, miracles involve God occasionally intervening in the regularities of reality.[1]

Hume's perspective has many problems, and I'm not the first to notice this. These problems stem largely from his understanding of the world's causal relationships. (And that's doubly odd, because Hume criticized the idea we could perceive causation. But that's another issue.[2]) I had criticized the idea of "natural laws" earlier in *The Uncontrolling Love of God,* and I suggested we use the phrase "law-like regularities" instead.[3]

More importantly, the vast majority of people don't think about miracles like Hume did. They don't assume his worldview. They don't say, "Wow! God just interrupted the laws of nature to heal your blindness!" Or "Look, the regularities of reality were violated, so they offered me this unexpected job!" For these reasons (among others), I set aside Hume's definition of miracles.

I found a second definition in my research, and it distinguishes between the "natural" and "supernatural." This view assumes God intervenes in the world, apparently coming in from the outside the causal structures of life. It also assumes existence operates according to natural causes, occurrences, and regularities that God occasionally enters to bring about an outcome. In this view, the supernatural trumps the natural, and *voilà...* a miracle occurs.

The idea that miracles involve God's occasional supernatural interventions or control of creation obviously opposes the *God Can't* view. It not only faces problems that come from saying God does or can control others, it also assumes God isn't always already present and active throughout creation.

My decision not to define miracles as supernatural interventions also came from Scripture. The Bible doesn't speak about miracles in this sense. Most biblical scholars don't think of miracles in this way. While I'm not chained to the language of Scripture, I follow its basic ideas.

I had no good reason to define miracles as "supernatural interventions."

A MIRACLE IS...

I had to fashion my own definition of miracles to write chapter eight of *The Uncontrolling Love of God.* I wanted my definition to agree with how biblical writers talk about miracles. It also had to fit with how most who witness miracles say today. And it had to sidestep all the problems with thinking God could or does cause or permit evil.

Here's the definition I settled on:

Miracles are unusual and good events that involve God's causal action in relation to creation.

Let me explain my definition's key aspects. Some people say all of life is a miracle. They believe everything that happens —

from the beautiful to the ugly, from the mundane to the momentous — is miraculous. They seem to say all occurrences in the world reveal God's will.

I don't think everything is a miracle. As used in the Bible and in most conversation, "miracle" describes unusual events, not just anything that happens. So in my definition, a miraculous event is *unusual*.

Second, the unusual events I consider miracles are *good* in some sense. I realize what's "good" or "bad" is partly subjective. Notice I said "partly," because I think there is an objective, God's-eye evaluation. We all consider some things good and others evil. It's what I call an "experiential nonnegotiable" in my writing. But my main point here is that I don't consider *every* unusual event a miracle. Torture is not miraculous, even though it's unusual in most contexts. Miracles are *good*.

Now to the last phrase: miracles involve God's *causal action in relation to creation*. I believe God is a real actor in the universe. To put it plainly, God is an omnipresent actor and necessary cause for every event in all of creation. (I'll explain this more in the next chapter.)

"God's causal action in relation to creation" also points to the causal capacities of creatures. I don't just mean complex creatures like you and me, dogs and dolphins. I also mean less complex entities in our world and those organisms that comprise our bodies. When I talk about the causal capacities of creation, I include atoms, quarks, and other tiny units of existence.

Miracles involve God's causal action in relation to all beings with casual force.

ALL THINGS ARE POSSIBLE?

God's causal action in relation to creation is conditioned by what's possible. God can only do what is *really* possible. That's part of the *God Can't* message. When Matthew records Jesus saying, "With God everything is possible," this can't mean everything *literally*. After all, other biblical passages say God can't do some things (e.g., can't lie, be tempted, grow tired, deny himself). God can't choose to stop existing or become Satan. And so on.

We creatures cannot do many things. We are limited, socially located, and finite. God calls creatures to do what is *really* possible. God never asks us to do the impossible, but what's possible can sometimes surprise us.

I can't resist commenting on a verse I often see pasted on T-shirts: "I can do all things through Christ who strengthens me" (Phil. 4:13). This translation lends itself to becoming a motivational speech: "Nothing can stop you from fulfilling your dreams!" But it also sets us up for failure. Not even God "can do all things," and we can do far less than God!

The verse fits nicely, however, with the idea God is a necessary cause for the actions of all creation. God provides us with might — the power to act — in each moment. We can act, because God enables us. A better translation of this verse might be, "I can only do the things I do because Christ enables me." Stick that on a T-shirt!

Back to miracles: It's important to consider what is truly possible if we want to understand miracles. In each moment, God responds to each creature and situation by providing new possibilities for action. God does this for complex creatures, simple creatures, and the smallest entities of existence. Each set of new possibilities is relevant for each being in each situation.

God sees all the options given our circumstances, relationships, facts, and data. God takes into account all the causes, factors, and actors in us and in each situation. Then God offers pertinent possibilities for action and empowers us to respond. God's enabling makes our response possible. God calls, commands, persuades, and inspires creatures of all complexities to choose the best among the possible.

All of this means — and this is so important — that miracles involve *both* God's initiating action and creaturely responses or the conditions of creation being conducive. For miracles to occur, God's initiating and empowering action is necessary. It's the primary causal factor. But God cannot bring about miracles alone. Miracles require creaturely cooperation or conducive conditions where cooperation is not possible.

LAWS, AGENTS, AND INANIMATE OBJECTS

Notice that my definition of a miracle does *not* say, "God breaks the laws of nature." From a *God Can't* perspective, God never interrupts the law-like regularities of existence, such as suspending the force of gravity. God never interferes with creation processes, such as interrupting the process of photosynthesis. Creation's regularities and processes emerge naturally from God's steadfast love. Because God always loves everyone and everything and God's love is relentless, law-like regularities naturally develop. For God to interrupt the law-like regularities that result from divine love, God would have to deny God's nature. And God can't do that.

When I talk about the creaturely aspect of miracles, I distinguish between "cooperation" and "conducive conditions." This distinction builds from what philosophers of science call "animate" and "inanimate" creation. I find most plausible a worldview that says organisms from the most complex to the simplest have the capacity to respond to God and others. But I don't think inanimate objects can respond. Inanimate aggregates like rocks, water, and metal don't respond like organisms can. Rocks don't have agency, for instance, like worms do.[4]

When miracles occur in relation to organisms and animate creatures, we say they cooperated with God's offer of unusual and good possibilities. But I'm not saying inanimate objects like rocks and water freely respond to God. Inanimate aggregates can be aligned, located, conditioned, or formulated so that God perceives what's possible and acts in relation to them and other creatures to present the possibility for miracles.

I'm not saying God can singlehandedly arrange inanimate objects to build a steel wall, for instance, and instantaneously stop a bullet. But given what's possible in any situation that includes inanimate objects, God does the best given what's possible. God can call organisms to use their agency in relation to inanimate objects, for instance. Or the response in one place can trigger a chain reaction that affects inanimate objects.[5] But there is no guarantee a miracle will occur. And because of the regularity among inanimate objects and aggregates, miracles among them are exceedingly rare.

This distinction between agent cooperation and conducive conditions among inanimate objects helps answer a question many ask: "Why do miracles occur far more often among people, agents, and organisms than among inanimate objects largely determined by nature's law-like regularities?" To ask the question differently, "Why are creature miracles more common than creation miracles?"

The answer: agents, organisms, and animate creation can respond to God's possibilities. The most complex creatures entertain more possibilities than simpler entities, but all animate creatures have some capacity for response. By contrast, inanimate objects don't respond. They are organized as inanimate masses rather than responsive individuals. And the law-like regularities emerging from God's steadfast love restrict the range of possibilities in their environment.

MIRACLES AND SCRIPTURE

I've offered a definition of miracles while addressing briefly issues in philosophy of science and divine action. Let's turn to the Bible. Does what I'm saying match Scripture?

In previous books and essays, I've discussed various biblical accounts of miracles. Writers of scripture use various words when talking about miracles, and those words are interpreted as wonders, signs, powers, energies, and more.[6] Some miracles involve complex or simpler agents, such as healings, exorcisms, resurrections, insights/revelations, salvation, and more. Others involve inanimate creation, such as Moses parting the Red Sea, Jesus feeding 5,000, walking on water, floating ax heads, and more.[7] I'll not rehearse the cases here that I've addressed elsewhere. Instead, let me make an overarching claim...

I know of no passage in the entire Bible that contradicts my definition of a miracle.

To put it differently, I know of no passage that says miracles require God to control creatures or creation. No story or passage of Scripture explicitly says God singlehandedly brought about some miraculous result.[8]

Most biblical miracle stories explicitly mention the actions of God and creatures. They describe creaturely response (e.g., "Your faith has made you well" [Mt 9:22; Mk 5:34. 10:52; Lk 8:48, 17:19, 18:42]) or the conditions of creation (e.g., "water stirs" [Jn 5:4]). Most miracles involve agents: people, animals, angels, organisms, and cells. My understanding of miracles fits these Bible stories well. Some miracles involve inanimate objects and aggregates. My understanding of miracles fits those too, but those conditions of creation must be conducive.

Several biblical passages support my claim that creatures can stop miracles from occurring. Particularly interesting are those that say God does not heal everyone or cannot heal at all. Jesus goes to his hometown of Nazareth, for instance, and cannot do miracles. The Nazarenes didn't cooperate. Other passages speak of Jesus healing many, but not everyone. One recounts how Jesus spit on dirt, put it in a blind man's eye, and the blind man received partial vision. So Jesus tries again. Examples such as these suggest various factors, actors, agents, and forces play a role in miracles.

Without cooperation, miracles cannot occur.

Admittedly, a few Bible stories mention only God acting. A miracle occurs, but there's no mention of creaturely cooperation or the conditions of creation. Sometimes, only God is mentioned as healer. For instance, the writer of Exodus quotes God saying, "I am the Lord who heals" (15:26).

Many believers encounter miracle passages in which only God is mentioned and *assume* God singlehandedly brought about the miracle. But is this assumption warranted?

When we read Scripture, we should ask, "Does a miracle story that only mentions God *explicitly* say there was no creaturely cooperation or contribution?" As I read the Bible, I can't find any passages overtly saying God alone brought about some miracle. In fact, I know of no verse — from the creation of the world, to the hardening of Pharaoh's heart, to the resurrection of Jesus, to other miracles, and to the eschatological end — that explicitly says God alone brought about some result.

Some readers of *God Can't* ask me specifically about God hardening Pharaoh's heart. They wonder if in this story God controls others. When we read the story carefully, we may notice biblical writers say God hardened Pharaoh's heart *and* Pharaoh hardened his own heart (Ex 7:13; 8:11,15,32; 9:34).

I agree with eminent biblical scholar Terence Fretheim when writes, "an act of hardening does not make one totally or permanently impervious to outside influence; it does not turn the heart off and on like a faucet." "Divine hardening did not override Pharaoh's decision-making powers," he adds.[9]

Pharaoh's heart hardened because he negatively reacted to signs from God. These signs originated in God, so writers rightly portray divine action as playing a role. But God did not control Pharaoh with these signs; Pharaoh decided how he would respond to them. Pharaoh's responses played a necessary role in the hardening of his heart.[10]

I find another set of biblical stories interesting. These stories describe something good and unusual — some even use the word "miracle" — but never mention God. The classic Old Testament story for this is the book of Esther. Even more interesting is the story of Peter healing with just his shadow, with no mention of divine action (Acts 5:15). Handkerchiefs and aprons bring healing and exorcise demons, but the writers never mention God working (Acts 19:12).

How should we interpret these "Godless" passages?

The vast majority of theologians think God was active in those biblical miracles that don't mention God. These theologians say God was working alongside creaturely agents, forces, and factors. When Esther miraculously saves her people or Peter's shadow heals the sick, God was a necessary cause in these good and unusual events. I agree.

But... if for theological reasons we can assume God was active but not always mentioned in biblical miracles, why can't we for theological reasons assume creatures were active but not always mentioned in biblical miracles? Assuming God and creation *always* play roles in miracles resolves mysteries and offers a plausible framework for understanding God's action in the world.

The Bible as a whole supports my theory of God and miracles.

CAN GOD TRY HARDER?

When pondering miracles (or the lack thereof), some will ask, "I know you're saying God can't control, but why doesn't God try a little harder?"

Those who ask this question assume God voluntarily chooses a particular degree of influence. The questioner thinks 0% means God is inactive, and they know I reject that view. And the questioner thinks 100% means God controls others, and they know I reject that. They assume God influences somewhere between 0% and 100%.

I think God always influences at 100%. But loving at full capacity is never controlling. To put it another way, 100% of divine action never singlehandedly determines outcomes. 100% of God's influence is 100% uncontrolling love!

The (wrong) idea that God chooses how much to influence triggers what I've called "The Problem of Selective Miracles." This problem comes when thinking God controls others when doing miracles. But the idea also emerges if one thinks God voluntarily regulates how much to influence.

A God who either controls or doesn't always influence fully would be responsible for both miracles that *don't* occur and prayers for healing *not* answered. The uncontrolling love of God view overcomes these problems by saying God can't control and always influences at 100%.

In *The Uncontrolling Love of God*, I added the word "special" to my definition of a miracle. I said miracles involve God's special action in relation to creation. Some readers assumed by "special action," God sometimes decides to be *especially* influential. I understand how traditional theological views influence readers toward these assumptions.

I use "special action" to say God's action toward creation involves responding by presenting to each unique possibilities. It's special, in that sense, because God's action is tailored to each creature. A God who is not relational can't respond in this special way, because a nonrelational God is nonresponsive. (See model five in *The Uncontrolling Love of God* for a description of a nonrelational God). So "special" action doesn't mean more or less; it means divine action suited to the situations, abilities, and possibilities for each creature in each moment.

To summarize, the God of uncontrolling love always loves at 100% capacity. This God never works part time or goes into semi-retirement. When miracles occur, it isn't because God put in a little extra effort. God always loves at full throttle.

DON'T BLAME THE VICTIM

The uncontrolling love of God perspective says creatures must cooperate or the conditions of creation must be conducive for miracles to occur. Someone might encounter this view and think, "People who are not healed must fail to cooperate with God." That person might say to a cancer victim, "You're not co-operating with God, because you're not getting better."

I strongly reject this "blame the victim" approach. But given what I've said, I can understand how someone might jump to this wrong conclusion. Let me explain why sick and hurting people who cooperate with God are not always healed.

A wide variety of causes, organisms, and agents com-prise our bodies. These entities often cooperate with one an-other, their environment, and God. But sometimes they don't. Sometimes cells go rogue, muscles atrophy, arteries clog, chemicals go out of balance, and so on.

Our minds influence but cannot control our bodies. Right now, my conscious mind is exerting powerful influence over my fingers as I type. But if I consciously will that my heart stop beating, it will continue. I don't control my heart. I know my mind can't control my body, because I've been trying for years to think my way to growing more hair!

The ill and hurting may consciously say "Yes" to God's heal-ing. But aspects of their bodies do not cooperate with God. The cancer victim may pray, act, and do everything she knows to cooperate with the healing God wants. But she cannot single-handedly prevent her cells from becoming cancerous. Organs, cells, muscles, and more in our bodies may not cooperate or be aligned for the healing God wants.

An uncontrolling love view of miracles does not blame victims for their suffering. What we do really matters. But we can't control our bodies. Those hurting often consciously say "Yes" to God, but their bodies don't cooperate or conditions aren't conducive to healing.

MATERIAL-MENTAL MONISM

Some readers will want to go deeper into miracles and uncontrolling love. This will mean studying issues in the philosophy of science, theology, scripture, and metaphysics. I encourage those who explore those issues in depth to investigate what philosophers often call "panpsychism." Allow me to whet your appetite for this deeper dive.

Panpsychism comes in many forms. At its root is the idea all existing things — even the fundamental units of reality — are neither merely bits of matter nor mental ideas. Instead, mentality and materiality are present in all creatures.

I call my panpsychist view "dual-aspect monism" or "material-mental monism." I believe every being in existence — from quarks to the most complex creatures — is comprised of both material and mental aspects. This makes responsiveness possible among even the smallest animate entities of existence. And complex responses — even conscious responses — can occur among complex creatures like you and me. My material-mental monism model and the more general panpsychism view answers tough questions humans have asked for centuries and ask today.

The material-mental monism model fits well in an organismic worldview. It also fits theologies that say God is relational, creatures have freedom, and the future is undetermined. It provides a framework for thinking God acts at all levels of creation without controlling any, because it assumes creatures of all complexities have some measure of agency to respond well or poorly to God's calls.[11]

When I first encountered panpsychism, I was skeptical. Later I understood it to solve what philosophers call "the mind-body problem." But I considered it then part of a technical discussion reserved for professional philosophers. In recent years, I've realized how panpsychism — especially material-mental monism — helps us understand God's providence in general and miracles in particular.[12]

IF GOD IS UNCONTROLLING, HOW DO WE EXPLAIN MIRACLES?

Let me conclude by returning to our initial question: "If God is uncontrolling, how do we explain miracles?"

I believe in miracles. Miracles are good and unusual events that involve God's causal action in relation to creation. They're not entirely in our heads; they're not entirely "in the eye of the beholder." But miracles also don't require God's intervention in creation to bring about a surprising result singlehandedly. And they're not supernatural interruptions.

Miracles can occur as God acts to empower, offer possibilities, and inspire creatures and creation. God works at the tiniest levels, among our bodily members, alongside our minds, and throughout the entire universe. When creatures cooperate, or the conditions of creation are conducive, miracles can happen.

Although God can't control, miracles can occur.

CHAPTER THREE

What does an uncontrolling God do?

Most God Can't *readers can answer this chapter's question...* at least partially. They might want me to clarify or expand on what the uncontrolling love view says about God's action. But most know the God described in *God Can't* always acts but never controls.

Those who interview me or come to public lectures are most likely to ask this chapter's question. If God can't prevent evil singlehandedly, they wonder, "Does God do *anything*?" Others hear me say, "God can't...," and think, "God isn't involved; we're on our own!"

This chapter explains how God always acts without controlling.

GOD IS LIKE US OR NOT?

Some people — especially scholars of religion — try to ignore this chapter's question. They set aside questions of divine action completely. Some ignore them to avoid controversy. Others claim to study only religious practices, ideas, histories, or phenomena. Some separate their own study of religion from what religions actually say God does, which sometimes is bizarre.

I have friends who say we can't know *anything* about God's actions. They claim God is *altogether* different from creatures. If God *is* different in every way, however, nothing we say, do, think, or imagine describes God. Even saying, "God doesn't act" says too much.

I call this "God isn't anything like us" view *absolute apophatic theology*. It offers nothing positive or constructive. According to it, God's actions aren't like ours in any way, so asking what God does is foolish. God is to this theology what a black box is to science.

I have trouble understanding why anyone who embraces absolute apophatic theology would believe in God. What is there to believe *in*? Besides, everyone I know who claims they can't know what God does, in reality, acts as if they do. They play theological cops to tell the rest of us we're wrong!

I reject the "God isn't anything like us" view. It runs counter to what most of the Bible says. It runs counter to how we worship, pray, and speak. We can't accept it and claim God is loving. And so on. There's no point to absolute apophatic theology... except to say to any positive claim about God, "Wrong!"

Others say God acts almost exactly like we do. In this view, God has a body like us but bigger. God has arms, feet, hands, legs, mouth, eyes, and so on. This view says God is just as morally unstable as we are. The "God is just like us" view claims God does both good and evil, remembers some things but forgets others, started living and will someday die, or something similar.

I sometimes call the "God is just like us" view absolute anthropomorphism. This fancy label means "a form like humans." But according to this view, God is just like us in other ways. God is made in our image.

I don't believe God is just like us or nothing like us. It's not all or nothing; there's a middle ground. To use the technical words, God is transcendent in some ways and immanent in others, because God differs from us in some respects and is similar in others.

GOD IS A UNIVERSAL SPIRIT WHO ACTS

It's difficult to point to obvious examples of God acting. A believer and unbeliever can see the same event and interpret it differently. The main reason we cannot clearly identify divine action is this: God is a universal spirit we cannot perceive with our five senses.

Biblical writers often speak of God as a "spirit." The common Hebrew word is *ruach*, and the Greek word is *pneuma*. These writers also say God is present to all creation. We cannot escape an omnipresent Spirit. My favorite phrase to describe this says God is a "universal spirit without a localized body."

English translations of *ruach* and *pneuma* vary, but scholars often translate them as "breath," "wind," "soul," or "mind." When used to describe God, these words suggest that God can't be seen but does influence creation. We might say we cannot perceive the universal Spirit with our five senses, but this Spirit affects us and everything that exists.

During the twentieth century, many compared God's unseen but influential presence to the 'ether' in the universe. Others compared God with gravity: an influential force we can't see, taste, touch, or smell. Today, some compare the universal Spirit with dark matter and dark energy.

Analogies between God and creation have limits, of course. One limit is that wind, breath, ether, gravity, and dark matter are not literally omnipresent. We can imagine a place in which the wind is not blowing or rocks without oxygen. We can imagine a gravity-free zone. And so on.

Comparing God with wind, gravity, and dark matter has another shortcoming. These forces don't have free agency, aren't personal, and don't engage in giving-and-receiving love. Wind and gravity aren't intentional; dark matter doesn't respond; air doesn't make choices.

Pneuma and *ruach* can also be translated "mind" or "soul." Describing God as a mind fits better with believing God is relational, personal, or an agent. Minds are affected by others, especially brains. They take in new information, experience emotions, and remember the past. John Wesley and others called God "the soul of the universe." Just as the soul or mind animates the body, God animates the universe.[1]

Saying God is a "universal spirit who acts" better describes God's universality and agency. As a universal Spirit, God is present to all creation. God acts in relation to the most complex societies and the least complex entities. As an agent, God has intentions, makes decisions, and loves. God acts and reacts, gives and receives, influences and is influenced.

God acts as a universal and agential spirit.

WHERE IS GOD?

Some people experience evil and ask, "Where is God?" Most don't expect to be given GPS coordinates. But they assume God can act in the world and wonder why God didn't prevent their suffering. I think the question, "Where is God?" should prompt us to wonder if God's acting can be observed.

Good biblical, theological, and philosophical reasons exist to think we cannot perceive God with our five senses. It's common to say God is "invisible." But we also cannot taste, touch, smell, or hear God, at least in the literal meaning of these sensory capacities.

There are also good biblical, theological, and philosophical reasons to think God is present to all creation. Being "omnipresent" doesn't mean God *is* all things. That's pantheism. It means God is present *to* all things.

Few consider what it means to believe God is omnipresent and yet not perceivable with our senses. It means, for instance, we can't look out of a window to see God walking outside. Not only is God omnipresent and invisible, God is also incorporeal. God doesn't have a body located in a particular place. Biblical passages that suggest God has a body (e.g., Moses looks at God's back [Exod. 33]) should be interpreted metaphorically, not literally.

We can't put God under a microscope and say, "There's God bouncing around the tiniest units of reality." Scientific experiments can't put an omnipresent God in one place and creaturely stuff in another. No research project could put creation influenced by God in one test sample and creation uninfluenced by God in another. If God is present to all creation, there's no way to isolate God from creatures for observation.

I once talked about God with a woman in Lake Tahoe, California. After some dialogue, she said, "I'd believe God exists if he parted the clouds and showed his face." She assumed God had a body and face and could be in one place and not others. She didn't seem aware God is an invisible spirit present to all creation.

The universal Spirit who acts does not watch from a distance, removed from the fray. God doesn't sit on the sidelines. But neither is God the impersonal Force in Star Wars. The universal Spirit intentionally acts and responds... creating and sustaining the universe through persuasive love.

DOES GOD CAUSE?

I think God acts as a causal agent. Sometimes philosophical language helps us talk about God. So let's go philosophic to explain what I mean when I say God acts as a causal agent. Don't let the word "philosophy" intimidate you! I'll try to keep things understandable.

Philosophers identify many kinds of causes. Perhaps the most common is the "efficient cause." Many have this in mind when they talk about "cause and effect." Efficient causes are what much of contemporary science emphasizes.

An efficient cause is the impact of one thing upon another. Think of a football player's body exerting impact — an efficient cause — upon another player. Think of the woman who slaps a man's face. That slap is an efficient cause. Water cuts through the stone using efficient causation, even though this work may take centuries. Even mist exerts efficient causation, albeit in more subtle ways. Efficient causation involves a physical dimension, even if our five senses cannot perceive that physicality.

A second cause goes by the name "final" cause. This label doesn't mean the last cause in a series. Instead, final causes are lures or attractors. We identify a beautiful car as a final cause when we say, "That car calls out to me!" We might be "drawn to" an attractive person, and in this, the person is a final cause. Final causes persuade, attract, or lure us toward possible action.

A third kind of cause is a "formal cause." These causes are possibilities, opportunities, forms, and ways of being. The possibility I might have coffee tomorrow is a formal cause. The opportunity I have to exercise today is a formal cause. Notice these causes are not exerting impact on me in the way an efficient cause does. Formal causes suggest actions I might take, arrangements to which I might conform, practices I might pursue, or ways I might exist. They are possibilities.

The uncontrolling love view considers God a universal spirit who acts as an efficient cause, attracts like a final cause, and offers formal causes as possibilities. As a spirit with being, God influences everyone and everything moment by moment. In this influencing, God calls, persuades, commands, or woos us to choose particular courses of action and ways of being. This is God's causal action.

Just as invisible gravity influences us, an invisible God also influences us. Just as our invisible minds influence our bodies, so the invisible Spirit influences the world. Although we cannot perceive God with our five senses, we can directly perceive God through our minds and bodies.

Theologians of yesteryear thought we had "spiritual" or "divine" senses with which to perceive God. I'm not suggesting that. I think we perceive God directly through nonsensory perception. If you care about the details, I've explained this view in various academic publications.[2]

The universal, invisible Spirit who acts has a physical aspect. To put it another way, God has both a mental and physical dimension. We cannot see these dimensions, nor can we taste, hear, touch, or smell them. But the God with a physical and mental dimension exerts causal influence on creatures with physical and mental dimensions. This is partly why I earlier proposed "material-mental monism." (Return to the last chapter for more information on that.)

Although invisible, the omnipresent Spirit exerts causal influence in diverse ways.

A NECESSARY BUT NOT SUFFICIENT CAUSE

Let's look at two other kinds of causes. The first is what philosophers call a "sufficient" cause. A sufficient cause brings about results all alone. It determines outcomes unilaterally and therefore, in itself, explains an outcome fully. The word I use to talk about a sufficient cause is "singlehanded." A sufficient cause *singlehandedly* generates a result.

Having introduced this cause, let me make a bold claim: I don't think sufficient causes ever occur. In other words, I doubt *any* being or force ever fully controls others. I know of no examples of sufficient causes ever occurring in the world. And from the uncontrolling love perspective, not even God can be a sufficient cause. A main point in *God Can't* is that a loving God cannot singlehandedly control others to prevent evil.

Neither creatures nor the Creator can act as a sufficient cause.

In light of the absence of sufficient causes, let's look at what philosophers call "self-causation." This label points to the causal capacity each creature has for itself. In complex creatures, self-causation is what we normally call "free will" or freedom. In less complex creatures, self-causation is a creature's agency or spontaneity. Even the simplest entities possess self-organization, which is also a form of self-causation. Self-causation is present in all existing things, from the most complex to the most simple.

From the uncontrolling love perspective, God necessarily provides self-causal powers to creatures in each moment of their existence. Freedom, agency, and existence are gracious gifts from God. God's love motivates God to self-give and others-empower moment by moment. But no one — not even God — can entirely remove self-causation from others.

This brings us to the last cause I want to explore. It's what philosophers call a "necessary cause." This is a cause required for something to happen or exist. For example, the union of sperm and egg is a necessary cause for you to exist. Oxygen is a necessary cause for the existence of water, because water necessarily requires two parts hydrogen and one part oxygen. Food, in one form or another, is necessary for creatures to live.

The uncontrolling love of God view says God is a necessary cause in the existence of *everything*. Without God's moment-by-moment creative activity, there would be nothing. God creates and sustains all things in relation with other causes and factors, so being a necessary cause *in* all things does not mean being the primary cause *for* all things. Although God is a necessary cause for the existence of all things, God is never a sufficient cause.

GOD IS A CAUSE AMONG OTHER CAUSES

Did God create you? Or did your parents?

The best answer to these questions is "yes." I don't mean it's a paradox. I mean creating involves multiple causes. In this example, your parents couldn't create you without God's action. But an uncontrolling God can't create you without your parents' actions.

It takes (at least) two, baby!

The idea our lives required both divine and creaturely causation may seem obvious. But some theologians reject it. They worry this makes God "one cause among many," to use their expression.

Bishop Robert Barron raised this worry during the 2020 COVID-19 pandemic. He was responding to New York Governor Andrew Cuomo, who said humans, not God, stopped the virus from spreading. "Underlying [his statement]," said Barron, "is the view God is one competitive cause among others. [Cuomo thinks] there's all the causality we affect in the world. But alongside that, there's the fussy intervening causality of God. [I believe] God is not one fussy cause among many."

Much of what Barron says in his several minute response fits the uncontrolling love view. He says, for instance, God *and* humans worked to combat the virus. He rejects the idea of God intervening, and he says God enables humans to act. But unlike Barron, the uncontrolling love perspective believes God is one cause among many.

What Barron thinks at stake when saying God is "one cause among many" emerges when he recommends how we should think about overcoming the Coronavirus. We should say, "We did it," he says, "and God has *everything* to do with it." Barron says, "We should say in regard to this and anything else, 'Oh Lord, it was *you* who has accomplished all that *we* have done.'"[3]

You did all *we* have done? What's going on?

Saying God is not one cause among many leads to confusion. This claim makes it impossible to know whom we should praise or blame. To say God "accomplished all that we have done" sounds like God acted as a sufficient cause.

It makes no sense to say God did it *all* and creatures did *some*. Imagine saying, "She did it all, but I helped." If you helped, she didn't do *it all*. There were multiple causes: your causation alongside hers.

The problem with saying "God isn't one cause among many" remains largely hidden when good things happen. God gets *all* the credit. "It's all God," a diva might say in response to praise and applause. And we might think, "She's humble, after all." Giving God *all* the credit means we get none.

If God is the *sole* cause of good, however, we are wrong to say, "Thank you," to those who help. No need to thank the chef; God did it. We should not express gratitude to those who sacrifice for our sake; it was all God. From this view, it's nonsense to say "Thanks!" to a teacher, medical worker, garbage collector, computer technician, or police officer. Any good they seemed to have done was, in Barron's view, fully accomplished by God.

The problem with saying, "God is not one cause among many" becomes more obvious when tragedy, abuse, and other evils occur. If, as Bishop Barron says, God "does it all" and "accomplishes everything," we should blame God for evil. God did it.

God "does it all but is not one cause among many" is how some theologians weasel out of conceptual conundrums like the problem of evil. "God's causation isn't like ours," is what they're saying. That's just a sophisticated way to play the mystery card. It removes any responsibility from God.[4]

My overall point: we should say God is one cause among others. God is not an exception to the basic rules of causation. God has unique causal functions, of course. God provides opportunities to creation, for instance. And God is the only causal individual who exists everlastingly. But God can act in these uniquely causal ways as one cause among others.

God and creatures affect what happens in life. When we experience goodness, we should praise God for being its source. But we should also thank creatures who cooperated with God. When outcomes are evil, we can blame uncooperative creatures, random events, or the conditions of creation. God did not want this evil, and creatures and creation sometimes oppose God's work for good.

Saying God is one cause among others makes better sense.

SUPERNATURAL, INTERVENTION, ALMIGHTY

Although I mentioned "divine intervention" and "supernatural" in previous chapters, it seems wise to address them here. I also want to explain what I mean when I say, "God is almighty."

"Intervene" means to "come into" or "come between." It comes from the Latin word *entervenio*. When used with reference to God, it gives the impression God comes into a situation from the outside. "Intervention" portrays God *over there* and entering a causal relationship *right here.*

The uncontrolling love perspective says God is always present to all creation. So it makes no sense to say God "intervenes" from over there. God is never away on holiday or out for a jog. God is always directly present as a necessary cause in every creature's life and every entity's existence.

The word "supernatural" also has problems. Some use this word to say God acts in the natural world. If that's all "supernatural" means, there's no bigger supernaturalist than me! But most people use the word to say God's actions are entirely unlike any natural actions in the world. To them, there's "natural" and "supernatural" activity. Those who claim the supernatural occasionally trumps the natural are usually saying God controls creation from time to time.

I refrain from using "intervention" and "supernatural" because in my experience, these words confuse rather than clarify. But I do talk about God's powerful causation, so I look for other words to describe divine action.

The three most common words used to describe God's power are "omnipotent," "sovereign," and "almighty." What these words mean depends on how one defines and uses them. In my experience, people use "omnipotent" and "sovereign" to say God directly or indirectly controls creation.[5] For this reason, I avoid using these words.

I prefer the word "almighty" to describe God's power. No word is perfect, of course. For some people, "almighty" has the negative connotation of "divine control." When I say, "God is almighty," I don't mean God controls! But I prefer "almighty" because it's what most English translators of the Bible use when describing God's power. And I like to use the "al" and "mighty" in the word to express my own view of divine power.

I believe God is "almighty" in three senses. First, God is mightier than any other. God has no equal in power. Second, God exerts might upon all others. God is a necessary but not sufficient cause upon all that exists. Third, God is the source of might for all others. Because of God's loving empowering, in God we live and move and have our being.

The way I define "almighty" fits with the idea God cannot control. God can be more powerful than any other and yet be unable to control anyone or anything. God can exert power upon all and yet cannot control any. And God can be the source of power for everything without singlehandedly determining anything.

I reject "all or nothing" ways of talking about divine power. Saying "God influences" is better, and I sometimes use that phrase. But in my view, all creatures influence, so "influence" doesn't distinguish God's action from creaturely action. The three meanings of "almighty" I offer allow us to make this distinction.

God is a uniquely powerful cause among other causes in the universe.

CAN AN ALMIGHTY GOD STOP TWO-YEAR-OLDS?

Those who first encounter *God Can't* sometimes ask, "If it's loving for us to stop evil and we sometimes can do so, why isn't it loving for God to stop evil?"

To answer this question, let's imagine a two-year-old walking freely toward a hot stove. And let's imagine you are standing near the child. Sensing a looming disaster, you grab the child's hand just before it hits the stove.

Did you express love in this action? I think so. And stopping the child would be loving if God could do it. Why can we sometimes stop a two-year-old from freely burning her hand, but God cannot?

The answer to this question returns us to what we explored earlier: God is a universal spirit without a localized body. God is incorporeal. This means God doesn't have a localized body with appendages. There is no literal divine hand to grab a two-year-old walking freely toward a hot stove.

The uncontrolling God of love is the source of all power and goodness. That's part of what I said it means to be almighty. And God necessarily gives freedom to complex creatures like two-year-olds. When you prevent a two-year-old from burning herself, we might say you act as God's metaphorical hand. Insofar as what we do as localized creatures is good, we as individuals and communities act as God's symbolic body.

Stopping a two-year-old from touching a hot stove, however, isn't the same as controlling her. You didn't act as sufficient cause. While we may sometimes be in the right place to use our bodies to stop evil, this doesn't mean we're controlling *every* aspect of the situation or people involved. Our capacity for bodily impact doesn't mean we singlehandedly determine outcomes.

When I think about bodily impact that doesn't control, I think about my daughter. While pursuing my master's and doctoral degrees, my wife gave birth to our three girls. When my middle daughter was going through the "terrible two" stage, she *hated* when my wife slipped off to work without saying goodbye. My wife did this if she thought the girls were sleeping. She didn't want to wake them.

When my middle daughter became aware her mother was gone, she'd throw a tantrum. She'd jump out of bed and run down the hallway to our front door. She'd pound her little fists, cry, kick, scream, and flail about. I tried all types of discipline to stop these tantrums. None were successful.

One particular morning, my daughter threw another tantrum. In frustration, I responded by doing what I don't recommend other parents do. I ran down the hall and picked up my two-year-old. I shook my finger in her face and said, "You will not throw a temper tantrum!" I then marched her back to her bed, as she screamed, hit, and kicked.

Arriving at her bed, I wrapped one of my arms to pin down her flailing arm. I put one of my legs over her kicking legs. And I put my hand over her mouth to muffle her screaming. I was doing my best to constrain a two-year-old throwing a tantrum!

In that moment, this thought ran through my head: "I can't control a two-year-old!" And then I thought, "Why should I think a bodiless God who gives free will can control others?"

I guess this story illustrates a second point: I do theology at the weirdest moments!

THE LOVE PROPOSAL

A philosopher named Arthur Holmes once criticized the general view I've been proposing. To be fair, he didn't know my *particular* view. He may have liked it. But Holmes argued the God process theologians describe cannot act.[6] Apparently, he thought a God who does not unilaterally determine others must not act at all. William Lane Craig made a similar mistake when he read my view and thought I was advocating deism![7]

In this book, in *God Can't*, and in many others, I explicitly say God acts. I think God's causal activity occurs everywhere, all the time. This is not deism. But I also deny God can singlehandedly bring about results. God can't control.

To illustrate how one can act without controlling, I want to repeat an illustration I used in *God Can't*. More than 30 years ago, I took my girlfriend to a special dinner. After the meal, I reached into my pocket, pulled out a ring, and asked her to marry me.

I acted. I did something. No outside forces or factors controlled me. I freely asked my girlfriend to marry me.

We were not engaged, however, until she accepted. She needed to act in response to my action. She could accept my proposal or reject it. Our possible engagement required not just my action but hers. I can act, and yet the outcome I want requires someone's positive response.

This analogy fits God's action. I believe the universal Spirit acts at every level of existence, all the time. This action includes God's causal effects, as God empowers, inspires, calls, and more. God is an efficient and final cause that provides formal causes. But because God always loves without controlling, God's actions require positive responses for the results God wants to see.

God cannot singlehandedly bring about the outcomes of love. God requires creaturely response. These responses come not only from complex creatures like you and me but also dolphins, ducks, dandelions, dendrites, and the smallest units of reality.

Because God loves everyone and everything, God needs creaturely collaboration.

WHAT DOES AN UNCONTROLLING GOD DO?

We can now answer this chapter's question: What does an uncontrolling God do?

God acts, moment-by-moment, in relation to all creation. God's action is real causation, an efficient and final cause that provides formal causes to everyone and everything. Although God is a universal spirit without a localized body, God exerts physical and mental influence upon others. God is a necessary but never-sufficient cause in creating all things. We rightly call God "almighty," yet God is incapable of controlling anyone or anything.

We live and move and have our being in the uncontrolling God of love. We rely upon this active Spirit for our existence and for the power to choose and act. God is the loving but invisible One who lures us toward beauty, truth, goodness, and overall well-being.

That's what I call action!

CHAPTER FOUR

What does it mean to say God loves everyone and everything?

I could write a book on each question framing these chapters. But it would take a long book — likely two long books — to cover last chapter's topic well. And this chapter? I'd need at least three books for all I want to say!

Readers of *God Can't* and *The Uncontrolling Love of God* already know that I think theology's orienting concern, central point, or primary motif ought to be love. I explain love briefly in those books and talk about its implications. But readers understandably want more, so they send questions.

Some readers ask specific questions: "Does God love cancer?" "Does God love rapists, murderers, and torturers?" "Does God love the Devil?" "Does God love the coronavirus?" And more.

Other questions are general. "Can you explain your defini-tion of love?" "Does God's love differ from ours?" "Does loving someone mean endorsing everything they do?"

I've written several books on love and edited others. If you'd like to explore how I define love, try *Defining Love: A Philosophical, Scientific, and Theological Engagement*. If you prefer theology, see *The Nature of Love: A Theology*. For a short and accessible book, see *Science of Love: The Wisdom of Well-Being*.[1] Even these books don't capture everything I want to say, so I have plans to write another!

WHAT IS LOVE?

"Love" may be the least defined among the most frequent-ly-used words in the English language. There are reasons for this, but I won't address them here. Instead, let me move to the definition of love I find most helpful:

> To love is to act intentionally, in relational response to God and others, to promote overall well-being.

The definition has three main phrases, and I want to ex-plain each briefly. The "intentional action" aspect says those who love act on purpose. Loving isn't accidental; it isn't hap-penstance. Love is a free and intended act. Those whose ac-tions unintentionally result in good do not love. We say a person tried to love based primarily on her motive to promote well-being, not primarily on the outcome of her actions.

I *don't* say love is a feeling. I'm not opposed to feelings, and I think love often if not always involves emotional and feeling aspects. Feelings play a major role in nearly every decision we make. But sometimes love requires us to act for good despite feelings pulling us in other directions. We may feel hate, disgust, or indifference toward someone, for instance, but we choose to love by acting for their good.

The second phrase says love involves response. We live in relationship with others, and those relationships affect us moment by moment. We're affected by our environment, histories, culture, situations, bodies, and so much more. We are relational creatures in an interrelated universe.

God is one among many actors and factors to whom we respond. As God acts moment by moment, God calls us to respond to the possibilities we encounter. We can respond properly or improperly. When we respond well, we love. As St. John put it, "We love because God first loves us" (1 Jn 4:19).

Those who love act intentionally in relational response to God and others.

The last phrase of my definition points to love's goal: well-being. Love doesn't act for the well-being of one or a few at the expense of the whole. It seeks *overall* well-being, even as it often focuses on particular goods in light of the common good.

Some people think a loving person has only the well-being of others in mind. But this perspective of love doesn't account for appropriate self-love. By contrast, my definition assumes self-love is part of acting to promote overall well-being. If we ought to love those whom God loves, we ought to love ourselves!

Love sometimes requires self-sacrifice, of course. We sometimes act for the well-being of others to our own detriment. At other times, we may have our own well-being primarily in mind as we promote overall well-being. When I brushed my teeth this morning, I had my well-being primarily in mind, although this self-love has positive implications for others (pleasant minty breath). In an interrelated world, the common good and my good often but not always coincide.[2]

When I say love promotes "overall" well-being, I'm not talking just about humans. "Overall" includes nonhuman creatures, plants, and smaller entities. It includes dimensions that are not just emotional, but also psychological, intellectual, social, economic, spiritual, and ecological. I even think our actions affect God's well-being!

I use "well-being" to capture what others mean by different words. Philosophers use *eudaimonia*, flourishing, or the common good. Theologians and biblical scholars use words like *shalom*, abundant life, or blessedness. In popular culture, we find words like happiness, fulfillment, or health. At their best, these words point to what is good.

Love aims to do good.

OUR LOVE IS LIKE GOD'S, GOD'S LOVE IS LIKE OURS

I think God's love is like our love. God acts intentionally, in relational response to others and God's own past actions, to promote overall well-being. My definition of love applies to divine love and creaturely love.

Most Christian theologians exempt God from their definition of love. Actually, few take the time to define love at all. That only leads to confusion. When theologians *do* offer a definition, many say creaturely love looks like "X," but God's love looks like "Y."

In most theological frameworks, divine love differs in kind from creaturely love. Comparing God's love to ours is like comparing apples and oranges, they may say. But apples and oranges are probably more similar than any similarity these theologians think exists between divine and creaturely love. Mysteries abound!

Christians who think God's love differs from ours rarely say so explicitly. But it becomes obvious when someone says, "God allowed her rape for His loving purposes." Or "God's love is tough; it sometimes kills." Or "God loves the unrepentant so much He sends them to Hell for eternity." Acts of love in these cases differ little from acts of evil!

Scripture generally points to a God who loves everyone and everything. I say "generally," because not *every* biblical passage reveals God as perfectly loving. I've read the Bible! Some stories and statements *do not* portray God as consistently loving. But I do think the overall drift of Scripture points to a loving God.

Let me put this another way...

After decades of studying Scripture, I've come to believe biblical passages that portray God as unloving are in error. It may seem bold to say this. But it seems the most honest. I don't look at biblical passages that portray God as violent, cock my head, squint, and say, "God killing people must be loving from the divine perspective." Instead, I say, "The biblical writers who think God kills people misunderstand God."[3]

It's not that I think I'm smarter than everyone when I say some biblical passages are in error. I say so because those passages don't fit the overall drift, big picture, or tenor of the *whole* Bible. I evaluate passages in light of the overall message, which I think portrays God as always loving. Passages that portray God as unloving don't fit the clearest revelation of God in Scripture: the life, teachings, death, and resurrection of Jesus.

And they don't match our deepest intuitions or what it means for God to be perfect.

What counts as loving is true for God and for us. While the overall drift of Scripture points to a God of perfect love, some passages don't. I'm comfortable saying passages that portray God as unloving are in error. What is love for God is love for us and vice versa.

LOVE COMES FIRST IN GOD

Although my love definition applies to God and creatures, divine love differs in scope, duration, and necessity. These differences are in modes and degrees, not in definition.

For instance, as a universal spirit, God directly loves everyone and everything. Localized creatures like you and me can't love everyone and everything directly. God has been expressing love for others everlastingly. Creatures started to love in history. God by necessity loves, because God's nature is love. You and I don't have natures of love, so we must choose whether to love moment by moment.

I could add additional ways God's love differs in mode or degree but not in definition. These similarities and differences fit the overall drift of the Bible.

For various reasons, I think love is God's primary attribute. As I said previously, love is logically prior among attributes in the divine nature. By "logically prior," I mean we should understand who God is in light of love. Where other divine attributes might seem in conflict with love, we should rethink those attributes.

In his commentary on 1 John chapter four, John Wesley argues for the primacy of love in God. When Wesley reflects on the famous phrase "God is Love," he says, "God is often styled holy, righteous, wise; but not holiness, righteousness, or wisdom in the abstract. God is said *to be* love, intimating that this is his darling, his reigning attribute, the attribute that sheds an amiable glory on all his other perfections."

Wesley rejects the idea God predestines people to Heaven or Hell. He thought a loving God would not use power in this controlling kind of way. A God in whose nature love comes first is more worthy of worship than a God who controls all things.

DOES GOD LOVE CANCER AND THE CORONAVIRUS?

If God loves everyone and everything, does God love rapists and arms dealers? Does God love torturers and embezzlers? How about cancer and the coronavirus? Does God really love *all* creation?

Answering these questions returns us to the question framing this chapter and to my definition of love. Lovers act to promote overall well-being. To apply this understanding of love, let's begin with God's love for rapists, arms dealers, torturers, and embezzlers.

Some use the word "love" to describe approval, affirmation, or pleasure in what others do. For them, "love" is similar to "like" or "desire for." But as I defined it, love acts for good. This sometimes means acting for good despite what others do.

God loves rapists, for example, because God acts for their well-being. But God doesn't like rape. God knows what's good for the rapist involves him avoiding rape, and that's obviously also good for the potential victim.

We can apply this principle to everyone. God loves us no matter how mild, severe, or shameful our sins. God opposes what undermines well-being. But God wants the well-being of everyone, even those who commit heinous and destructive crimes.

Let's apply this principle to God's love for other actors and factors in existence. God loves all cells, for instance, even those that become cancerous. Rather than destroying them, God works to heal unhealthy cells. In every moment, God acts, invites, and offers opportunities for well-being at all levels and complexities of existence.

God also loves viruses, even the coronavirus. Unfortunately, many hear "virus" and assume such entities are intrinsically evil. This is not true. The vast majority of viruses make the world a better place. Most viruses promote overall well-being by enhancing species diversity, for instance. Less than 1% of viruses cause overall harm.

God calls, guides, or inclines cancerous cells and destructive viruses toward what promotes health. Sometimes, cells and viruses malfunction, mutate, or act in ways that harm. God works to restore and heal when they go awry. When creatures, entities, or creation fail to respond well to God's loving action, God doesn't destroy them. God forgives and "turns the other cheek" in the effort to get them back on track to promoting what is good.

This principle is helpful to keep in mind when we think about treating one another. Rather than killing or destroying those who harm, we ought to work to heal, transform, and rehabilitate. Since all of us have done harm, we're just doing unto others what we — as those who sometimes do evil — want done to us: loving them.

GOD'S RESPONSIVE LOVE

Saying God responds to cancerous cells, destructive viruses, rapists, arms dealers, and to all who harm implies that creation affects its Creator. To put it another way, God *receives* from creation. Readers of *God Can't* may have noticed I claimed that God not only self-gives and others-empowers but also receives and is affected. God is relational.[4]

I like to call the idea God gives and receives the "theo-logic of love." This idea will sound obvious to most people, because we know love is relational. Biblical writers also describe God this way. God engages in giving and receiving love.

Some important theologians have *not* adopted the theo-logic of love. They believe God is unreceptive, unrelated, and uninfluenced by the world. In their view, God has no emotions, and we make no difference to God's experience. Let me give two examples.

Thomas Aquinas is perhaps the most influential systematic theologian in history. Aquinas thought God was benevolent toward creatures. But he rejected the idea God received from creatures.

"A relation of God to creatures is not a reality in God," says Aquinas.[5] God knows creatures as ideas without being causally affected. Creation never *actually* influences God, but relations "ascribed to God only in our understanding."[6] In other words, Aquinas thinks we only imagine God gives and receives in loving relationship. He cannot see the theo-logic of love.

Or take Anselm, another early church theologian of great importance. Here's how Anselm talks about God's compassion, which is obviously a form of love requiring God to be influenced by creation. "How are you compassionate God and, at the same time, passionless?" asks Anselm of God in a prayer. He doesn't think God has any emotions. But he knows that if this is true, it makes no sense to think God is compassionate.

Anselm goes on to say to God, "If you are passionless, you do not feel sympathy. And if you do not feel sympathy, your heart is not retched from the sympathy for the wretched, but this is to be compassionate." Anselm is saying we need emotions and passions to feel sympathy. And compassion requires sympathy. "But you don't have either passion or sympathy," says Anselm to God, "so how can we call you compassionate?"

Anselm answers his own question: "When you behold us in our wretchedness God, we experience the effect of compassion, but you do not experience the feeling of compassion. Therefore, you are both compassionate because you do save the wretched and spare those who sin against you, and also not compassionate, because you are affected by no sympathies for wretchedness."[7]

Like Aquinas, Anselm concludes that we only *think* God is compassionate. God is not actually so. The idea God is compassionate is just in our minds; it's not *actually* true of God. By the way, if you think it's strange for Anselm to ask God a question and then answer the question himself, let me explain. A God who never receives and is unaffected by creatures *never* responds to prayer. So Anselm must respond to himself!

The theo-logic of love rejects the nonrelational ideas Aquinas and Anselm endorse. This theo-logic says God's love is giving and receiving. Just as others affect our love relationships, God is also affected. This is another way the definition of love I offer applies both to creatures and the Creator.

DOES GOD *CHOOSE* TO LOVE?

One idea in *God Can't* says God's eternal nature is love. Among other things, this means God must love, because God can't deny God's own nature. You and I choose whether we will love, because we don't have eternal natures of love. These claims lead to questions like these:

Is freedom an aspect of love?

If God doesn't freely choose to love, how can we say God loves?

In my view, God necessarily loves. We could say God is not free not to love. Because love comes first in God's nature, God does not freely choose whether to love us. In this sense, divine love is not free.

Divine love is free in another sense, however. God freely chooses *how* to love. God acts moment by moment moving into an open future, and God sees all possibilities. Consequently, God freely and creatively chooses how to act in light of these possibilities. God can't know with certainty how creatures will act or how the future will play out.[8] So God has freedom in each moment to love in particular ways God believes will promote overall well-being.

We might put it this way: the fact *that* God loves everyone and everything is necessary. But *how* God chooses to love is contingent upon what's possible and the relationships God has with each creature. Notice these views also fit my definition of love. While it's God's nature to love, God chooses how to act intentionally, in relational response, to promote overall well-being. God's love transcends creaturely love by being necessary without being entirely different.

WOULD GOD LEAVE US, FORSAKE US, OR STOP LOVING US?

I often hear people say, "God can sovereignly choose to do whatever he wants!" This statement indicates these people think power comes logically before love in God's nature.

If true, this means God could freely choose to stop loving us. God could choose to leave us or forsake us. The God for whom power comes before love can turn us into robots, withdraw from us permanently, or act as a devilish rascal!

We have little reason to trust a God for whom love comes second.

Most people who say God can sovereignly do whatever he wants don't believe God may choose to stop loving, leave, or forsake us. They think God will be faithful. I've come to think most people who talk about God's "sovereign choice" actually *don't* think God can stop loving us. They haven't worked through their fundamental beliefs to make them consistent.

To explore the hierarchy of love and power in God, I like to ask people three questions.

1. *Could* God leave us, forsake us, or stop loving us?

Many people answer this question, "Yes." They think it's possible for God to choose to be unloving, and God could freely leave us and forsake us. In their view, God can sovereignly choose to do whatever he wants. I disagree, of course.

Let's call this view the "voluntary love" perspective. I hear it often. It says a sovereign God can choose to do whatever is compatible with divinity. It says God voluntarily, not necessarily, loves creation. Again, I disagree.

Let's move to the second question.

2. *Would* God leave us, forsake us, or stop loving us?

Just about everybody answers "No" to this second question. They think God will always be present, love, and support us. But why should those who think God can choose to stop loving us think God won't decide to do so? On what grounds should we trust a God in whom power comes before love?

Let me put it this way: those who say "God can sovereignly choose to do whatever he wants" have no grounds for trusting that God will love, remain with, and never forsake us. In fact, perhaps God does not love some people. Perhaps God has not loved in the past. Perhaps God is a mean, ornery devil, at least sometimes!

Let's go to the third question.

3. *Why* do you think God would never leave us, forsake us, or stop loving us?

Most people answer by saying something like, "That's just who God is." Or "We can trust God." "If God left us, forsook us, or stopped loving us," they might say, "God wouldn't be acting like God!" Or some variation of these answers.

When answering this "why" question, most people appeal to their deep belief about who God is. This deeper belief shows most people think God *is* necessarily loving, essentially relational, and not in the business of forsaking us. People may not articulate well this deep belief. They may say, "God must be God." But many actually think God must love, because it's God's nature to do so.[9]

Deep down most people *don't* think God can sovereignly choose to do whatever.

I use these diagnostic questions to show that many people *actually* believe love comes first in God's nature. Some may talk about "God's sovereignty" and say, "Don't limit God!" But when the "why" questions of love are asked, many say God must be God and can't be otherwise.

Many believers have inconsistent views of God's love and power. Incoherent theology is prevalent. Some people recognize the need for consistency and choose power over love. This theology of sovereignty typically makes God the author of sin and one who either causes or allows evil.

Other believers revel in their theology's inconsistency. They take it as proof God's ways are above ours. Or they claim incoherence allows more room for the Spirit to move. But in actual practice, inconsistent theology grants personal authorities and authoritarian systems dominant power. This irrational theology is a ready tool for a power-hungry prophet or the privileged who want to maintain the status quo.

The mystery card of theological inconsistency doesn't help us much.

The uncontrolling love of God perspective chooses the consistency of saying love comes before power in God's nature. God *can't* sovereignly do whatever we can imagine. Consequently, we can trust God to love everyone and everything all the time. The uncontrolling God of love consistently opposes evil and acts to promote overall well-being. And because love comes first, this God cannot leave, forsake, or stop loving us.

DOES GOD NEED OUR PITY?

I recently engaged in an academic discussion with a theologian named Kevin Vanhoozer. Kevin read portions of *The*

Uncontrolling Love of God. An academic book published his response and my response to him.

One of Kevin's criticisms was striking. It relates to my solving the problem of evil. Kevin worried my solution might make God less transcendent and not worthy of worship. Here are his worries in question form:

"If Thomas Jay Oord is right, is the God who is uncontrolling love more deserving of our worship or of our sympathy?"[10]

In my response, I argued that the God of uncontrolling love *is* worthy of worship. I worship this God unreservedly and wholeheartedly, and so do many others I know. But Kevin's comment prompted me to think carefully about what vision of God provokes my worship.

I've come to believe it's actually psychologically impossible for me to worship a God who could prevent evil but fails to do so. After all, I don't unequivocally respect humans who fail to prevent evil when doing so was possible. So I can't unequivocally worship a God who can prevent evil but chooses not to do so. I may be afraid of such a God. I may dread this God or worry about his punishment. But I can't unreservedly love and worship such a being.

The God who allows evil is unworthy of my worship.

Kevin wonders if the uncontrolling God of love deserves our sympathy. By "sympathy," I assume he means pity rather than the philosophical meaning of sympathy. I don't think we should pity God.

These references to worship and pity remind me of a conversation I had with a fellow theologian. I was explaining my view that God is uncontrolling and can't singlehandedly prevent evil. My theologian friend responded and said he prefers a God who can control. He then smirked and said, "You know, Tom, your God is just doing the best he can!"

I thought about his remark for a second and responded, "True, my God is doing the best he can. But your God could be doing a whole lot more but apparently doesn't care enough to do so."

This conversation illustrates love as my fundamental theological intuition. When I think about a God worthy of my worship, I find more winsome the vision of a God who consistently loves but can't control than a God who can control but loves inconsistently.

Some theologians will claim the God they affirm both controls and loves consistently. But considering the tragedy, abuse, and other evils of our lives, that can't be the case. Those who claim God controls and loves consistently typically say it's a mystery how God does both. This measure of mystery undermines rather than enhances my worship. I'm unable to worship a God who cannot be understood to such a high degree.

I don't think I've figured out God completely. But it's difficult for me to understand what motivates people to worship a deity so incomprehensible!

Perhaps my inability to worship a controlling God points to a deficiency in my way of living. I doubt it. Perhaps it reflects my inability to think reasonably. I doubt this too. It may even point to a psychological flaw. I don't think so, but that's a possibility.

I find comfort in knowing others feel as I do. Many try to worship the God who sovereignly controls. But they can't get motivated in light of the evil in the world or their own lives.

How much more beautiful and glorious is a God who loves everyone all the time?! How much more majestic is a God whose power is shaped by love?! How winsome is the God present to all creation, not only creating and influencing, but being influenced as an expression of love?! How much more worthy of worship is the God who cares about you and me and every living thing in all of creation?!

The God of uncontrolling love motivates me to worship!

WHAT DOES IT MEAN TO SAY GOD LOVES EVERYONE AND EVERYTHING?

I've offered various answers to the question that frames this chapter. I began with a definition of love that says to love is to act intentionally, in relational response to God and others, to promote overall well-being. This definition applies both to God's love and creaturely love.

Love comes first in God's nature. This means God's love differs from ours in scope, mode, and duration. We must choose to love, and our love is limited. God loves by nature but freely chooses how to love in each moment.

God loves everyone and everything. But that doesn't mean God endorses everything that occurs. God can love cancer and the coronavirus, because God acts for their well-being. God can love rapists and torturers without approving of their dastardly deeds. God loves all creation without liking some of what happens in the world.

God loves everyone and everything by acting for the well-being of all.

CHAPTER FIVE

How does Jesus fit in a theology of uncontrolling love?

Jesus Christ is central to **God Can't** *and the uncontrolling love of God perspective.*

A person doesn't have to be a follower of Jesus to accept this perspective. I know people in non-Christian faith traditions who endorse uncontrolling love ideas, some who identify with no religious tradition, and others who consider themselves in two or more religions. But Christians are especially attracted to *God Can't* proposals.

Of the questions I'm answering in this book, the Jesus question is the least likely to be asked of me. Most people readily see connections between Jesus and uncontrolling love. But to some, the connection isn't clear.

This chapter does not answer every question about Jesus nor does it develop a fully-orbed Christology. Instead, I focus on how Jesus reveals God's love to be uncontrolling.

THE LOVE OF JESUS

John begins his gospel with these words, "In the beginning was the Word, and the Word was with God, and the Word was God" (Jn 1:1). Christians wrestle with the exact meaning of these words, but they agree John believed Jesus was this "Word" who was "with" and "was" God. Jesus tells us something essential about the divine.

In John's first letter, he makes this simple but profound claim, "God is love" (1 Jn 4:8, 16). Jesus helps us understand what this love means. "In this way the love of God was revealed to us," John writes, "God sent his only Son into the world so that we might have life through him" (1 Jn 4:9).

Matthew, Mark, and Luke bear witness in their gospels to Jesus' love. His life, words, ministry, death, and resurrection are for the sake of creation. Jesus healed the sick, preached the good news, ate with sinners, ministered to the poor, wept over the dead, encouraged the downhearted, and showed compassion. Jesus stands as the fullest revelation of God's loving nature and activity.

Jesus' suffering and death on the cross reveals God as one whose love includes being affected by others. "God proves his love for us in that while we were still sinners Christ died for us," says the Apostle Paul (Rm 5:8). "God was in Christ reconciling the world to himself," says Paul (2 Cor 5:19). Because of this, we can "know the love of Christ," even though it "surpasses" full understanding (Eph 3:19).

There is little doubt that Jesus points to a God of love. But does he point to a God whose love is *uncontrolling*? Can we gather from Jesus' life, words, and ministry that God *can't* control creatures or creation?

I think Jesus *does* reveal God's love as necessarily uncontrolling. And I can marshal various biblical passages as evidence for this argument. But looking at a particular passage in Philippians might be especially helpful.

KENOSIS

I often draw from a song in the Apostle Paul's writings to explain my uncontrolling love view. It's found in a letter meant for Christians in the ancient city of Philippi. Before citing the song, Paul says the letter's readers ought to regard the good of others before or in addition to their own. Love often calls us to focus upon others instead of only upon ourselves.

To illustrate what love looks like, Paul quotes the song. Here's part of it...

> Let the same mind be in you that was in Christ Jesus,
> who, though he was in the form of God,
> > did not regard equality with God
> > as something to be exploited,
> but emptied himself,
> > taking the form of a slave,
> > being born in human likeness.
> And being found in human form,
> > he humbled himself
> > and became obedient to the point of death —
> > even death on a cross (2:5-8).

"Emptied himself" is one English translation of the Greek lyrics. Interpreters also translate kenosis as "self-giving," which is the translation I prefer. The song is saying Jesus took the form of a servant, humbled himself, and endured death on a cross. The point seems to be that love sometimes calls us to go to great lengths — even death — to promote overall well-being. We ought to follow Jesus' example.

After pointing to Jesus' example of self-giving love, Paul tells his readers to "work out your own salvation with fear and trembling; for it is God who is at work in you, enabling you both to will and to work for his good pleasure" (2:12b-13). He's saying God empowers us — "works in" and "enables" us — to express love. But we have to respond, to "work out" our salvation. Some Christians today use the phrase "prevenient grace" to describe God enabling us to love. God graciously acts first in each moment to empower and call us to respond.

Paul's overall argument seems to be that Jesus' life, teachings, and death reveal a God who engages in self-giving, others-empowering love. To put it simply, Jesus re-presents divine love. And this empowering love enables us to promote good and leads to what Christians often call "salvation."

KENOSIS CHRISTOLOGY

For much of Christian history, theologians have wrestled with formalized Christian statements — "creeds" — that try to describe Jesus' relation to God. Some creeds stated that Jesus was both human and divine. Jesus had "two natures" that were "communicated" in one person. How anyone could have two natures and yet be one person is a paradox. This paradox baffles to this day.

If we focus on what the Bible says about Jesus, we primarily see him as human. He didn't express the attributes many think God possesses. Jesus wasn't omnipresent, for instance.

He lived in Palestine, not everywhere in the universe. Jesus was not almighty, immutable, omniscient, and so on. He was an extraordinary person, but he didn't have the characteristics most think essential to deity.

Theologians sometimes draw from Philippians 2 to argue Jesus voluntarily set aside divine attributes to become incarnate. The claim Christ temporarily set aside divine attributes has been called "Kenosis Christology." It's controversial, in part, because it seeks to overcome the two natures paradox by emphasizing Jesus' humanity.[1]

In recent decades, kenosis discussions have shifted. Instead of pondering which divine attributes were communicated to Jesus and which were not, kenosis theology today typically explores how Jesus reveals God. Instead of speculating how Christ relinquished attributes when becoming a Nazarene, many now think of Jesus' kenosis as telling us something about who God is and how God acts.

I believe contemporary kenosis theology better accounts for Jesus' own witness and the Bible's broadest themes. The life, teachings, and cross of Christ powerfully reveal God's power as non-coercive love. Although Jesus did not have all the characteristics God does, Jesus' revelation of divine love makes him the "exact representation of God's nature," to quote the writer of Hebrews (1:3).

Just as Jesus self-gave for the good of others, God also self-gives for our good.

GOD NECESSARILY OR CONTINGENTLY LOVES?

While Jesus provides vital information about God, there are important differences between the two. Sorting out the similarities and differences is central to why Christians differ in their understanding of the one they call "Christ."

For instance, as a human, Jesus freely chose to love. At least that's what I think and many theologians agree. We believe that when tempted, Jesus could have yielded. Jesus could have sinned. He did not succumb to temptation but loved consistently throughout his life.

If Jesus could have sinned, he differed from God in a crucial way. Jesus did not have a nature in which love is logically prior to will. Although Jesus reveals a God who always loves, we can't know from him alone that God *necessarily* loves,

The Philippians song does not say God *necessarily* loves creation. The overall biblical witness does not require one to affirm God's necessary love, although one can make a strong case. Neither does the Philippians passage nor the overall Bible require us to think God *contingently* loves us. To argue God loves necessarily, we must make a case on other grounds.

To do something necessarily is to *have to* do it. A snake necessarily slithers; it's not a snake's nature to run a marathon. Saying God necessarily loves means God *must* love.

To do something contingently means it *may or may not* be done. A duck may waddle or fly; it's not a duck's nature to do just one or the other. If God contingently loves creation, God may or may not love us. A God whose love for creation is contingent decides to love one day but may decide differently the next.

I sometimes called my view "essential kenosis." I coined this phrase in response to the Philippians 2 passage and the "necessary or contingent" debate. Essential kenosis says God *must* love others, because it's God's nature to do so. Love for creation comes logically first among God's attributes. So God necessarily loves us, and God can't fail to do so. While God freely chooses *how* to love in each moment, God necessarily loves all creatures.

On what grounds, then, do I claim God necessarily loves creation?

AN ESSENTIALLY LOVING GOD WOULDN'T ALLOW EVIL

My claim that God necessarily loves us rests in part on solving the problem of evil. It rests on believing God's love is necessarily self-giving, others-empowering, and therefore uncontrolling. A God who always loves but can't control cannot singlehandedly stop evil.

Many theologians think God contingently loves creation. We see this most clearly when we read these theologians say God voluntarily self-limits to allow creation to love. Jürgen Moltmann, for instance, says God voluntarily "withdraws" for the sake of creation to "allow space" for creatures.[2] Roger Olson speaks of self-limitation in terms of God "permitting" creatures to act.[3]

I disagree with the idea God voluntarily self-limits for many reasons, but mainly because this view of God's love and power cannot solve the problem of evil. It says God allows evil rather than preventing it. Victims, survivors, and the abused can't trust a God who, as John Polkinghorne puts it, "is deliberately self-limited to allow causal space for creatures."[4]

I believe a perfectly good but voluntarily self-limited God — if this God existed — would become un-self-limited, in the name of love, to prevent preventable evil. Because genuine evils occur, I can't believe God is voluntarily self-limited. I think God's nature of love limits what God can do. And God necessarily expresses uncontrolling love for creation.

To see the problem with saying God contingently loves, we might apply self-limitation to other scenarios in life. Imagine a father who voluntarily self-limits to allow one child to kill another, when stopping this murder was possible. We wouldn't say this father loves necessarily. Imagine a mother who allows a neighborhood bully to molest her child. Mothers who don't prevent molestation when doing so was possible are not consistently loving. Or imagine a police officer who voluntarily self-limits to allow a rapist to do his dastardly deeds. This officer would not be doing her job, let alone expressing love. These people do not love others necessarily, because loving individuals don't allow evil they could prevent.

Let me summarize. While Jesus gives us our best portrayal of God's nature, he doesn't possess all the divine attributes. In his life, teachings, death, and resurrection, Jesus reveals God's love as self-giving, others-empowering, and uncontrolling. This is kenotic love. Essential kenosis comes from the additional speculation that God's love for creation comes logically first among attributes. Love for others is a necessary aspect of God's nature. So God must love and cannot control others. Although the Bible doesn't clearly say God necessarily loves us, given the problem of evil and the logic of love, we are safe to speculate that God is essentially kenotic.

God necessarily expresses self-giving, others-empowering, and uncontrolling love for all.

THE VIRGIN BIRTH

So much could be said about Christology from an essential kenosis perspective. I hope someday to write a book on the subject. But I want to look at particular examples of how Jesus reveals God's love as uncontrolling. I explore three issues some might think at odds with *God Can't* theology.

The first issue we might call "the Holy Spirit conception of Jesus," although it's what many call "the virgin birth." Usual explanations of this event assume God used controlling power. These explanations say God acted supernaturally to do this miracle singlehandedly. To put it another way, God acted as a sufficient cause to incarnate Jesus, either breaking the laws of nature or overriding creaturely actors.

We earlier explored the problem with thinking God controls others to do miracles. Why would a God who can do miracles singlehandedly not prevent genuine evils? But the belief God can control creatures or creation leads to other problems too. For instance, one wonders why the Bible would have errors, contradictions, and ambiguity if God could control its writers to produce a perfect text. The idea God can control also leads one to wonder why divine communication today is so ambiguous. It's hard to understand why a loving God would create through a long and painful evolutionary process if God has controlling power to snap existence into its present state and avoid all evolutionary evils. If God can singlehandedly reveal the right set of religious beliefs in a crystal-clear manner, why doesn't God do so? If God can singlehandedly stop the climate crisis and fix our planet, why doesn't God do so? But I digress.

This section focuses upon God becoming incarnate in the Holy Spirit conception of Jesus. Conventional theologies assume God supernaturally intervened to become incarnate as Jesus. They presume God needed to control creatures when doing this miracle. The virgin birth seems to many an obvious example of a time God must have singlehandedly brought about results.

What would an uncontrolling love view say?

When the angel visits Mary, he tells her she will conceive in her womb and bear a son whom she should name Jesus. She wonders how this could be possible, because she has not "known" a man. The angel responds, "The Holy Spirit will come upon you, and the power of the Most High will overshadow you." (I call this the "Holy Spirit conception.") Mary responds to the angel's words, "Here am I, the servant of the Lord; let it be with me according to your word" (Lk 1:26-38).

"Let it be with me."

Mary cooperates with the plan. Theologians who assume God can control often miss or at least under-emphasize her cooperation. Many read the story and assume the angel tells Mary what God has foreordained and foreknown. The uncontrolling love view says that without Mary's consent, the conception would not have occurred.

Of course, one could read this story of an angel talking to Mary as a mythical or metaphorical act. There are good arguments for this approach. To do so would mean sidestepping questions of divine action.

But what if we think the conception story tells us something true about the way God acts in the world? And what if Mary's cooperation plays an essential part of any adequate explanation of the special incarnation of God in Jesus? What if Mary matters?

The idea God needed Mary's cooperation aligns nicely with essential kenosis. This miracle occurred when a creature — Mary — cooperated with God. Just as important, the uncontrolling love view overcomes the worry that the Most High, the Holy Spirit, or an angel forced Mary to be the mother of Jesus. In other words, the *God Can't* view provides a framework to denounce the idea Mary was subjected to non-consensual impregnation.

The uncontrolling love view says the incarnation of Jesus was consensual.

So how did Mary become pregnant? Did the angel have sperm for Mary? Was this conception self-caused, in the sense that some creatures can self-fertilize and conceive? Was Mary pregnant from some other man? Is this a nonhistorical story characteristic of other stories circulating in that time told to associate Jesus with the divine?

The text does not answer such questions. But it does say Mary cooperated: "Be it unto me."

JESUS' MIRACLES

I covered an uncontrolling love view of miracles in a previous chapter. Here I want to show how Jesus' miracles fit the uncontrolling love perspective too.

Many miracle stories in the New Testament report Jesus saying to the healed, "Your faith has made you well." These accounts explicitly point to the role a healed person played in their recovery. The Greek word used in these instances is not limited to physical healing; writers also use it to describe spiritual healing. Christian traditions that emphasize our role in spiritual healing should naturally understand why physical healing involves creaturely cooperation.

In other Gospel stories, factors and actors beyond the one healed proved crucial. In one story, men dropping their paralyzed friend to Jesus through a hole in a roof. Jesus says the faith of the friends brought about the healing (Mk 2:1-5). A mother's persistence led to her daughter being cured (Mt 15:21-28). Even dramatic miracles such as Jesus saying "come forth" to Lazarus can be interpreted as involving both divine and creaturely action (Jn 11:43).

Some people believe *all* healing can be explained fully without appeal to God's actions. These people admit people sometimes get well. But they claim healing comes through luck, the placebo effect, natural causes, medical practices, or something other than divine activity.

The uncontrolling love of God view says *all* healing involves both divine and creaturely causation. Luck, the placebo effect, medicine, or natural causes may each play a role. But God's loving care was always influential. The Great Physician works with or alongside creatures and creaturely means. Sometimes healing does not occur because creaturely factors, actors, or conditions aren't cooperating or conducive.

The cooperative nature of miracles is especially clear when Jesus *can't* perform miracles. The classic case of Jesus being unable to do miracles is his hometown of Nazareth. St. Matthew says Jesus could not do many miracles there because of their unbelief (13:58). Mark reports that "all" the sick were brought to Jesus, and he heals "many," but apparently not all (Mk 1:22-24). John tells a story of Jesus healing a man at Bethesda. Although the man was surrounded by "many invalids — blind, lame, and paralyzed," Jesus healed the one and not others (Jn. 5:1-11).

Jesus *did not* walk around healing everyone singlehandedly.

Some readers of the Bible notice that Jesus did not heal everyone who needed it. They offer "explanations" for this selective healing that blame the victims, appeal to a mysterious divine plan, call the illness God's punishment, and more. Much more satisfying is the idea Jesus wanted to heal everyone but encountered actors, factors, forces, and agents that did not or could not cooperate.

In sum, Jesus acts to do miracles and his varied success suggests his goals of love require creaturely contribution and/ or conducive conditions in creation.

THE RESURRECTION OF JESUS

Let's move to the miracle many Christians think is most important: Jesus' resurrection. "God raised Jesus from the dead," say biblical writers (Acts 4:10; 5:30; 1 Cor. 6:14; Eph. 1:20; Heb. 13:20; 1 Pt. 1:21; Rm. 8:11). Jesus didn't self-raise; he didn't singlehandedly decide to come back to life. But many Christians think God had to control Jesus to bring him back to life.

Do biblical texts actually say God singlehandedly resurrected Jesus?

No, they do not. While many Christians assume God raised Jesus unilaterally, the writers of the New Testament don't explicitly say this. The assumptions of most Christians are based upon the often-unstated belief God can control anyone or anything.

Were other factors, forces, or actors involved in God's resurrecting? There are hints of this, and I'll point to them. But we don't have direct access to what occurred *as* God resurrected Jesus. There were witnesses after Jesus' resurrection, but no one was present during the decisive resurrecting activity.

An adequate explanation of Jesus' resurrection will involve a primary role for God's action: "God raises Jesus." The question remains as to what *other* causes, forces, factors, and actors were involved. The *God Can't* explanation says Jesus' mind/spirit/soul (depending on which word you prefer) and bodily members played a role in his resurrection.

It's not hard to imagine Jesus' mind/spirit/soul cooperating with God. Those who, like me, affirm continued subjective experiences beyond bodily death — what most people call "life after death" — will think Jesus continued having subjective experiences after his body died. Someone so in tune with God — "I and my father are one" (Jn. 10:30) — would naturally cooperate with God's resurrecting activity. Jesus' continually existing self would have strong reasons to cooperate.

We can also imagine elements of Jesus' body cooperating with God or being rightly aligned despite their damaged state. Jesus' body doesn't disappear into nothingness. We know from other resurrection accounts that dead bodies can revive without sufficient causes. The near-death experience literature offers many examples. Besides, a body dead for thirty-six hours in a cold tomb would not be entirely decomposed.

We find other intriguing factors and actors in stories about Jesus' resurrection. For instance, Matthew says an angel rolled away the stone from the entrance to Jesus' tomb (28:2). If God can singlehandedly raise Jesus, why send an angel to open the door? Interestingly, when Jesus raised Lazarus from the dead, he asked someone else to roll away the stone before calling to Lazarus to come forth. Did God do the same in Jesus' resurrection?

Consider also the high degree of ambiguity related to Jesus' post-resurrection sightings. The women who came to the tomb on the morning of his resurrection mistook Jesus for the gardener (Jn 20:14-15). His friends walking for miles alongside Jesus on the road to Emmaus don't recognize Jesus until he breaks bread (Lk 24:13-35). And so on.

A God who could singlehandedly raise Jesus and thinks witnesses to this resurrected man are important ought to make recognizing Jesus easy, obvious, and unambiguous. But that's not what we find in the text. This alone should make us rethink the idea God has the ability to raise Jesus singlehandedly and then exhibit the risen Lord unambiguously.

The most important argument for thinking God's raising Jesus was a cooperative venture comes from the logic of love itself. To many, love is obviously relational, persuasive, and uncontrolling. Love does not override, nor does it act in a vacuum. Love isn't a solitary activity. "Love does not force its own way" (1 Cor. 13:7).

To those who think God's activities are always loving, it's natural to think the resurrection of Jesus was not a controlling action. To put it another way, had God's raising of Jesus been a controlling act, it would not have been loving! Although many have not applied the logic of God's uncontrolling love to Jesus' resurrection, once presented, many find it makes good sense.

Others look to build from evidence and arguments that say God raised Jesus through love rather than control. The case based on evidence looks at the clues I've mentioned. They also consider other questions of life, the broad biblical witness, the problem of evil, and more. This approach involves building a case. I think the overall case for saying Jesus cooperated with God's resurrecting is strong.

As I mentioned earlier, I can find no scripture that explicitly says God singlehandedly controls others. The vast majority of biblical passages either explicitly or implicitly speak of both divine and creaturely activity when describing how any event occurred. No biblical passage unambiguously says God was the only actor in some event and there were no creaturely factors, actors, or causes. That includes passages that proclaim Jesus' resurrection.

HOW DOES JESUS FIT IN A THEOLOGY OF UNCONTROLLING LOVE?

Most Christians say Jesus reveals God. I agree. But many Christians also claim or assume Jesus sometimes used supernatural controlling power. The uncontrolling love of God view says we have good grounds to believe Jesus reveals God as expressing self-giving, others-empowering, and therefore uncontrolling love. Jesus shows this love in his teachings, miracles, death, and resurrection. Even the Holy Spirit conception required Mary's consent.

There's more to be said about Jesus and an uncontrolling love Christology. But those who wonder how Jesus fits in the *God Can't* view should now see fits nicely. In fact, Jesus provides our clearest picture of the God whose love is uncontrolling.

We need the revelation of divine love that Jesus re-presents today as much as ever.

CHAPTER SIX

If God created the universe, why can't God stop evil?

Sometimes Facebook rants make good discussion starters.

The lines below come from someone who has not read *God Can't*. The main point of his Facebook post poses a question many who read the book ask. And it frames this chapter's focus...

"If God created men, women, all creatures, and the universe in six freaking days, why is He so powerless to change the horrible things that happen on earth? He's freaking God!!! With a wave of hand, He should be able to end all this evil. I have to conclude God does not exist. Never has."

To put it simply, If God can create a universe, why doesn't God stop evil? This chapter answers that question.

A MERRY-GO-ROUND

Imagine that city officials commissioned a contractor to build a park for children. Officials told the contractor to include playground equipment, water features, game areas, hangouts, healthy food dispensers, and more.

Suppose when creating the park, the contractor put a merry-go-round at the center. But next to it, he posted signs saying, "Don't Play on This Merry-Go-Round!" "Off Limits!" "Stay Away!" And "KEEP OUT!"

When officials inspected the park, they wondered what was going on. "Why did you include a merry-go-round," they asked, "but warn children not to play on it?"

"I've designed this park to be loads of fun," answered the builder, "... except for this merry-go-round. Children must *not* play on it. If anyone does, I've designed the park so calamities will ensue. I've placed knives and sharp glass throughout, and these sharp objects will protrude from the ground the moment anyone plays on the merry-go-round. I've rigged areas of earth to open up, suck down, and suffocate children. The vending machine will begin offering methamphetamine and crack-cocaine. Loaded handguns will be distributed. Water fountains will periodically spout poison and acid. And if someone gets on the merry-go-round, every blond-haired child will be bullied."

Would we consider this man a *good* builder?

Many people think the creation story in Genesis presents a similar situation. They assume God (for some reason or another) decided to create a universe from absolutely nothing. Being unconstrained, God singlehandedly set up creation's playground: its systems, laws, causal structures, creatures, and possibilities.

The world God created was good... except for one tree. It bore fruit that, if eaten, brought about calamity. After creating this tree, God warned humans that death would come if they ate from it.

Humans couldn't resist the fruit. But eating it generated all manner of evil. Not only were these humans negatively affected, all creation thereafter suffered personal, social, mental, ecological, and natural evils. God created the world with dire consequences if even one person ate this forbidden fruit... that God created from nothing.

Should we consider a God who created a world and added features with great potential for calamity a *good* Creator?

We could also ask the question this way: Is there any difference between a contractor who builds a playground with a merry-go-round that if used, causes pain, suffering, and death and a God who builds a universe with fruit that if eaten, causes pain, suffering, and death?

THE PROBLEM AND MY ASSUMPTIONS

The Facebook post in question assumes nothing can thwart the Creator of the universe. This assumption seems safe, assuming God initially created the universe from nothing and can create from nothing today. If God faced no constraints when initially creating, God would solely decide the fundamental causal patterns, processes, and creaturely capacities. And this God could create more from nothing today. In fact, the God who brings something from nothing could, on a whim, send it all back to nothingness.

That's unlimited power!

So... why doesn't the God who can create from nothing prevent evil? Why doesn't this God instantaneously create barriers to stop the spread of the Coronavirus, for instance? Or create barriers to disease? Or create something out of nothing to stop rapists, murderers, and torturers? Or create obstructions that prevent freak accidents? And so on?

To answer these questions and the question that frames this chapter, I want to state my fundamental beliefs about God and creation. I doubt the four beliefs will surprise most readers. But I want to be clear about them.

1. God created the universe and continues to create today.
2. Creatures and creaturely factors can co-create with God.
3. God is perfectly good and always loving.
4. Evils occur that make the world worse than it might have otherwise been.

Let me also point toward my answer to this chapter's question. I believe we need to rethink what it means to say God created "in the beginning" and creates today. More specifically, we should believe our loving Creator *always* creates in relation to other actors and factors, which means God *never* creates singlehandedly or from absolute nothingness.

Even when creating, God's love is uncontrolling.

I REJECT CREATION FROM NOTHING

The Bible has many creation stories and statements about God and creatures creating. But most people look to the first chapters of Genesis when thinking about God's initial creating. The first lines of Genesis say this,

"In the beginning when God created the heavens and the earth, the earth was a formless void and darkness covered the face of the deep, while a wind from God swept over the face of the waters."

Although these verses do not say so, many Christians, Muslims, and Jews assume God created "in the beginning" from absolute nothingness. The Latin phrase for this idea is *creatio ex nihilo*: creation from nothing.

I reject the theory God ever or even could create from absolutely nothing. But I believe God created the heavens, earth, and every living and nonliving thing. If there are other universes besides ours — a "multiverse" — God created them too. In fact, I think God creates in every moment in relation to creation. And God's moment-by-moment creating activity is everlasting, without beginning or end.

The claims in the previous paragraph probably sound unfamiliar. I'm writing a full-length book to explain them, but I want to share some of those ideas here.[1] They can help us affirm God as Creator and yet believe God is not directly or indirectly morally responsible for evil. And they can help answer this chapter's question.

When I say, "I reject the idea God created from nothing," I mean "nothing" in the literal sense of the word. Some theologians say God created the universe from nothing, but "nothing" actually means "something" for them. That "something" may be chaos, unseen actualities, unformed matter, or something else. But it's "stuff."

I embrace the idea God created from creaturely "stuff." I sometimes use the word "scratch" to describe it, and I say God created our universe from scratch. But "scratch" isn't absolute nothingness. In fact, by "scratch" I mean something valuable, with inherent forces, and the potential to become something beautiful.

Rather than saying "something" is nothing, most theologians say they believe God created the universe from *literally* nothing. Nada. Zilch. Donut hole. Null set. Zero. In the view of most, God started creating roughly 13 billion years ago (or 10 thousand years ago, according to young-earth creationists) from *absolutely nothing*.

I disagree with those who say God created the universe from nothing.

PROBLEMS WITH THE CREATION FROM NOTHING THEORY

Believing God can create from absolutely nothing leads to a host of problems. Most people are unaware of those problems, so they don't question *creatio ex nihilo*. That's understandable. Unless we have reasons to question what we've been told, we typically accept it.

I began to question the creation out of nothing theory in the mid-1990s. The issues expressed in the Facebook rant first alerted me to some of the theory's problems. If God created the universe from absolutely nothing, God is ultimately responsible for the fundamental structures, laws, and possibilities of existence. If God can create something from absolutely nothing, God should create obstacles to prevent evil today. Because I believed evils occur that a loving God would want to prevent, I started to question *creatio ex nihilo*.

Over the years, I realized the theory had other problems. I briefly list nine below. You may think some problems are more acute than others. But seen in light of the whole, even less consequential problems contribute to the justification for rejecting *creatio ex nihilo*. I should note that although Scripture plays a central role in my theology, I placed the biblical problem last. It serves to transition to the next section.

1. The Theoretical Problem - Absolute nothingness cannot be conceived. It's intellectually impossible to fathom.

2. The Historical Problem - Creation out of nothing was first proposed by Gnostics. Gnosticism assumes creation is inherently evil, so a good God doesn't act in relation to creation. Most believers think otherwise.

3. The Empirical Problem - We have no evidence our universe originally came into being from nothing. While I affirm the Big Bang view of our universe, science doesn't tell us out of what the Big Bang came.

4. The Creation at an Instant Problem - We have no evidence that creatures or creaturely entities can emerge instantaneously from absolute nothingness. "Out of nothing comes nothing" is the old saying; *ex nihil, nihil fit.*

5. The Solitary Power Problem - Creation out of nothing assumes God once acted all alone. But power is a social concept and only meaningful in relation to others.

6. The Errant Revelation Problem - A God who can create something from absolutely nothing could guarantee an unambiguous, inerrant message. But an unambiguously clear and inerrant divine revelation does not exist.

7. The Evil Problem - If God once had the ability to create from absolutely nothing, God would essentially retain that ability. But a loving God with this ability would be morally culpable for failing to use it, at least periodically, to prevent genuine evil today.

8. The Empire Problem/Status Quo Problem - The power necessary to create from nothing supports the idea God causes or allows the establishment of empires and wants the status quo. People who see the need for social change think otherwise.

9. The Biblical Problem. The Bible does not explicitly support creation from nothing. Writers speak of God creating out of something, that that "something" might be water, the deep, chaos, invisible things, and so on.

CREATION FROM NOTHING IS NOT IN GENESIS

The first verses of Genesis don't say God created from nothing. I'm not the first to realize this. Many of the most influential biblical scholars say the idea God created from nothing is not in Genesis or elsewhere in the Bible.

Let me quote several...

- "Creation out of nothing is foreign to both the language and the thought of the unknown author of Genesis," says Claus Westermann. "It is clear that there can be here no question of *creatio ex nihilo*..."[2]
- "God's creating in Genesis one," says Terrence Fretheim, "includes ordering that which already exists.... God works creatively with already existing reality to bring about newness."[3]

- "Properly understood," says Jon Levenson, "Genesis 1:1-2:3 cannot be invoked to support the developed Jewish, Christian, and Muslim doctrine of creation ex nihilo."[4]
- "'Nothingness' is not the picture of the situation at the beginning," says Mark S. Smith. "Unformed as the world is, *tohu va bohu* is far from being nothingness or connoting nothingness."[5]
- "It can be said that Yahweh is the creator of the world," says Rolf P. Knierim, "because he is its liberator from chaos..."[6]

The list of Bible scholars denying that *creatio ex nihilo* is in Genesis is long. It includes liberal and conservative voices.[7] It's hard to overemphasize this point, so I'll say it again: Genesis 1 and 2 do not support the creation from nothing view.

The only verse in the Bible to mention God creating from nothing is 2 Maccabees 7:28, a book from the Hebrew Bible. If you've never heard of this book, you're not alone. This book is not found in most Bibles used by Protestants, because they don't recognize it as scripture. The verse comes from a passage in which a mother speaks to her son...

> She leaned over close to him and, in derision of the cruel tyrant, said in their native language: "Son, have pity on me, who carried you in my womb for nine months, nursed you for three years, brought you up, educated and supported you to your present age. I beg you, child, to look at the heavens and the earth and see all that is in them; then you will know that God did not make them out of existing things. In the same way, humankind came into existence (27-28).

Some claim the phrase "God did not make them out of existing things" refers to creation from nothing. But the context of the verse conflicts with this interpretation. The mother witnesses to bearing, nourishing, and educating her son. "In the same way, humankind came into existence" points to the role mothers play in creating and training. It's not talking about creating from absolute nothingness. A better analogy might be to say God created the heavens, earth, and humans in the divine womb. And even here, the sexual connotations lead a contemporary person to wonder what other factors were involved in the conception of creation in God's womb.

We find no explicit reference to *creatio ex nihilo* in New Testament writings. The book of Peter offers the most statement about God's initial creating. God created out of water and by means of water (2 Pt. 3:5). Other biblical passages speak of God creating out of "unseen things" (Heb. 11:3), un-grouped people (Rom. 4:17), and creation generally.

Early Christian and Jewish theologians believed God created the world out of something. Philo, for instance, postulated a pre-existent matter alongside God. Justin, Athenagoras, and Clement of Alexandria spoke of God creating the world out of something. Origin of Alexandria and later John Scotus argued God has always been creating. "These theologians," says historian Gerhard May, "could hold an acceptance of an unformed matter was entirely reconcilable with biblical monotheism and the power of God."[8]

While the biblical writers and early theologians did not affirm *creatio ex nihilo*, later significant Christian theologians did. In fact, most Christian theologians in the past and present embrace the creation from nothing view. Because it's important to consider the tradition when doing theology — important to me, at least — I do not oppose the majority flippantly. To my mind, however, the nine problems I listed are so strong that opposing the majority view seems wise. Besides, when I have a choice, I opt for what the Bible, experience, and reason suggest when they oppose the majority in the tradition.

A NEW THEORY OF INITIAL CREATION

Pointing out problems in the traditional view of how God created the universe is important. But it's not enough. A constructive Christian theologian like me should suggest a replacement.

I call my replacement *creatio ex creatione sempiternaliter en amore*, which is Latin for "God always creates out of creation in love." Here are the basic components of this alternative view.

Unlike many theologians, my view of God creating begins with God's eternal nature. I think God everlastingly loves creaturely others. "Love for creation" is necessary to what it means to be God. This means love is God's motive for creating and God has *always* been creating. God's loving nature is the ground for both God's initial and ongoing creating of our universe.[9]

We can understand God's creating by reflecting on the revelation of divine love in Jesus the Christ. John's Gospel says all things came into being through Christ, and without Christ, not one thing could come into being (1:3). If Christ is uncontrolling, and if God creates through Christ, God's creating is uncontrolling. I think God's creative love was uncontrolling "in the beginning" and throughout the roughly 13 billion years of our universe.

Let me respond to a potential reaction to this reasoning: If God once existed all alone and created from nothing (the view

I reject), some might say God's initial creating would not control others. No "others" would exist.

If *creatio ex nihilo* is correct, nothing existed prior to God's initial creating to *be* controlled. But if by "control" we mean, "be a sufficient cause" (see discussions in previous chapters), the God who creates out of nothing would control in this sense. God would be the only cause — which is a sufficient cause — in the first moment of our universe. If God has or can single-handedly bring about results, the problems of evil we often addressed arise.

My view that God always creates out of creation in love, overcomes the problem of evil and the eight other problems I listed. It says that even in the first moment of our universe — at the Big Bang — God created in relation to what God had created earlier. In fact, God always creates in each moment "out of" or in relation to what God created previously. And God has everlastingly been creating, which means there was no "first moment" in this causal chain.

If you're like most people, your brain blew a gasket while trying to comprehend the ideas of the previous paragraphs. So let me sum up what I'm saying to help you understand my view. I'm saying God creates all existing things in relation to what God created previously, creaturely factors, and actors. God's creating had no beginning. There was never a time God started from nothing. Because God's eternal nature is creative love, God has always been creating and loving creatures.

I tried to capture these ideas in my view with its label. Here it is again: God creates out of creation everlastingly in love. I recognize these ideas need further explanation. And there is bound to be some misunderstanding. So let me address a few of the most common misunderstandings I encounter.

SO... OUR UNIVERSE ALWAYS EXISTED?

When hearing me say God creates out of what God previously created, some wonder if our universe is everlasting. My theory rejects that idea. It affirms the notion that our universe began with a Big Bang. But it says the chaos of a previous universe came before the Bang. And God created our universe in relation to the one God previously created.[10]

God never creates in absolute isolation. God always creates in relation to creaturely others that also contribute to what exists. Those "others" may be complex creatures like you and me or quarks and other subatomic particles. God's creative love works with others even when creating.

While no universe exists everlastingly, a succession of entities, creatures, or universes always exists. The everlastingly creative God creates each creature and universe in this succession. Every creature is temporary, in this sense; all creaturely others have a beginning. And no universe is co-eternal with God.

No analogy can perfectly explain what I'm proposing, but let me offer something. Suppose Jim can live a million years. And suppose it's Jim's very nature to marry. Jim always has at least one marriage partner. But let's suppose each of Jim's partners lives an average life span of 80 years. So he goes through a succession of marriages — his nature is to marry — but none of his partners lives as long as he does.

Apply this analogy to God and creation. An everlasting God who by nature always creates and loves creaturely others will always have creaturely others. But none is everlasting; each comes and goes. The succession is everlasting, but no creature or universe is everlasting. In this way, God can always create out of what God previously created and yet no creature or universe exists everlastingly.

In sum, our universe — or any universe — is not eternal.

SO... CREATION PRE-DATES GOD?

To deny God created our universe from nothing might lead some to think creation exists before the Creator. My view denies this, however. It says God always creates in relation to or out of what God previously created. Let's speculate about what that might have been like at the Big Bang.

Whatever existed prior to the moment our universe exploded into existence must have been highly diffuse, chaotic, and simple. Those elements derived from the dying universe preceding ours and the indeterminate realm of possibilities in God. God also created these basic elements out of which God created our universe. In other words, God created something new at the Big Bang from that which God created before the Big Bang.[11]

My creation doctrine says God always creates in each moment out of that which God created in previous moments. This means no universe, no world, no creature, no "thing" preexists or predates God. My view agrees with a common view among theologians that God didn't create our universe out of "stuff" God had never previously encountered. God never "stumbles upon" something God had not first created.

God exists, loves, and creates everlastingly. But God relies upon creaturely others when creating. The activity of others plays an essential role in God's creative activity.

In sum, no universe, creature, or creaturely thing predates God.

SO... GOD NEEDS CREATION?

To say that God can't control others when creating but always creates in relation to creation sounds like God *needs* creaturely others. To some theologians, saying, "God needs..." is like saying a circle is square. They believe God has no needs whatsoever.

Some are motivated to accept *creatio ex nihilo* to safeguard their view that God does not depend upon creation in *any* respect. They prize independence and reject the idea creation influences God. To them, "God" = "essentially independent and without need."

I think God depends on creation in some respects but not others. I don't believe God needs creation for God to exist. God exists necessarily, so God doesn't depend upon creation in this sense. Ancient people used the word "aseity" to describe the idea God exists in God's self. God requires nothing beyond God's own being. I affirm divine aseity when defined this way.

I reject the idea "aseity" or God's necessary existence requires us to think God is independent in all respects. In previous chapters, I said God depends on creation in ways that pertain to love. Because God necessarily loves creaturely others and love is inherently relational, God necessarily relates to creatures. Relational love is never solitary. In that sense, God depends on creation.

My creation theory also says God always creates in relation to creation. This implies that creation and creatures play a necessary role in the existence of others. That's another way of saying God's love is uncontrolling. God depends in this sense upon creatures in the creative process. This dependence is not about whether God *will* create. God necessarily creates, and the motive to create comes from love. But the results of God's creating also depend upon creaturely forces, factors, and choices.

Saying God depends upon creation when creating overcomes the worry that God literally creates from God's own body. In other words, it rejects pantheism. Creatures depend upon God's initiating action in each moment, and they respond by joining, to whatever extent possible, the creative process. Creatures are created co-creators with God. My view is a form of panentheism.[12]

Love motivates God to create in relation to creaturely others whom God created previously. Because God loves, God needs others.

SO... GOD ISN'T FREE?

When explaining that God always creates out of that which God previously created in love, I've used the word "necessarily." I've said God necessarily creates, in the sense of *must* create in relation to creaturely others. If God necessarily creates, in what sense is God free?

We looked at the issues of divine freedom when we explored whether God chooses to love. The conclusions we embraced in those discussions apply here. Just as God does not voluntarily choose to love but does so by nature, God does not voluntarily choose to create. God creates by nature.

God *is free*, however, when choosing *how* to create, given the creaturely conditions and God's love. God freely creates in relation to creation and whatever is possible that would be loving. The future is open and not yet determined. God can't create something not possible to create, given the circumstances also generated by creaturely causes, factors, and actors. But God freely chooses while creating in relation to the past a yet-to-be-determined future.

Let me illustrate. Each of us is human, and we're not free to be otherwise. We can't breathe exactly like fish, for instance. We can't fly exactly like eagles. So our freedom is limited by what it means to be human.

We have a degree of freedom, however. Humans act freely in human ways, given what's possible in each moment. We're free to use scuba gear, fly airplanes, and more. These freedoms are contingent upon the circumstances. Two hundred years ago, no one was free to fly an airplane. Five hundred years ago, no one freely spent hours underwater with scuba gear. Our freedom is real, but because of our humanness and the conditions we face, it's limited.

Similarly, God is not free to be something other than God. To be God means having particular divine attributes and an eternal divine character. I claim God must create; God is not free not to create. But God is free to create in relation to creatures and creation given what's possible.

God's freedom is limited by divine love and relations inherent in love.

IF GOD CREATED THE UNIVERSE, WHY CAN'T GOD STOP EVIL?

Early in this chapter, I said a contractor built a park and merry-go-round with the potential to inflict unnecessary pain, suffering, and death. I questioned whether we should call this contractor "good." I wondered whether we should call "good" a God who created a world with the potential to inflict unnecessary pain, suffering, and death. This wondering arises if we believe God can create singlehandedly or from absolutely nothing.

The problem of evil cannot be solved if God created the universe singlehandedly or from absolutely nothing. For this reason (and eight others), I reject the view God ever creates from nothing. Instead, I believe God always creates in relation to creatures, creation, and creaturely forces. And God's creating is always loving.

Because when creating God cannot control others, God is not morally responsible for the pointless pain, suffering, and death in creation. God never started creating with a blank slate, and God can't control others. God isn't like the contractor who rigs a playground for evil. God began creating our universe in relation to forces, factors, and entities God could not control and in relation to possibilities for good and evil.

In love, the Creator God invites creatures to co-create. It's God's nature to do so. Creatures can use their creative contribution in positive or negative ways. A loving God cannot control what God creates alongside creaturely others.

CHAPTER SEVEN

What hope do we have if Gods love is uncontrolling?

This chapter's question explores hope for the afterlife and what theologians call "eschatology." Of course, "hope" is larger than those categories. But the questions I receive from *God Can't* readers focus on the afterlife and "end game" of existence.

In the past, I've called my view of these matters a "participatory eschatology." I coined this label, because it points to the role creatures and creation play when talking about hope. More recently, I use the label "the relentless love" view. I still believe creation plays an essential role in the work for a better future. But I believe we best answer our questions about hope when we center them on God's love.

The question for this chapter arises from a particular worry. We might put the worry like this: If God can't singlehandedly prevent evil, what hope do we have for love's ultimate triumph? Most who ask questions about the afterlife are concerned with their personal destiny or the destinies of those they love. "What will occur after we die?" they ask. But hope also has a cosmic or universal aspect. "What hope do we have that all creation will eventually be reconciled, redeemed, or made right with God?"

To those who understand what I called "indispensable love synergy" in *God Can't*, it's obvious our choices matter. Hope for a better tomorrow requires cooperating with God. But what about the afterlife? What happens to those who fail to cooperate? Does God send anyone to Hell, send everyone to Heaven, destroy some, or something else?

In this chapter, I focus on what hope for the afterlife might mean.

THE OLD TESTAMENT

The relentless love theory I offer — and the hope it provides — draws from the Bible. One doesn't have to believe the Bible tells the truth about all things to accept my theory. In fact, those in nonbiblical traditions or people who embrace no religion at all could embrace the relentless love view. Anyone who believes in God or something like the divine could, at least theoretically, affirm the hope expressed by my afterlife theory.

It surprises many people to discover that what Christians call "the Old Testament" has little to say about people going to Heaven or Hell. The common view in says dead people go to *Sheol*, which is the place of the dead. Ancient people considered this site an underground pit or cave. The writer of Job expresses this view:

> Are not the days of my life few?
> Let me alone, that I may find a little comfort

before I go, never to return,
to the land of gloom and deep darkness,
the land of gloom and chaos,
where light is like darkness (10:20-22).

According to biblical passages, dead people in *Sheol* cannot relate with God. The Psalmist describes this state as follows:

For my soul is full of troubles,
and my life draws near to Sheol.
I am counted among those who go down to the Pit;
I am like those who have no help,
like those forsaken among the dead,
like the slain that lie in the grave,
like those whom you remember no more,
for they are cut off from your hand.
You have put me in the depths of the Pit,
in the regions dark and deep (Ps. 88:3-6).

Old Testament writers occasionally speak of saints who fly straight into the heavens without dying. Enoch and Elijah are examples. But ordinary people — both believers in God and unbelievers, the righteous and unrighteous — go to the pit.

Ancient peoples believed generating descendants — having children — continued a person's influence after death. It was a blessing to be told, "your descendants will be many, and your offspring like the grass of the earth" (Job 5:25). Given this view, Old Testament writers encouraged procreation. Ancient peoples were most concerned about life ending prematurely.

Jewish ideas about life after death changed between the writing of the Old and New Testament books. Biblical scholars attribute this change to the widening relationships Jewish people had with other cultures. Among the new ideas to emerge was the possibility humans might be resurrected to an afterlife experience. The details of this view varied among teachers and traditions.

THE NEW TESTAMENT

The resurrection of Jesus is *a*, if not *the*, central event in Christianity. The New Testament books were written decades after his resurrection, but it's unlikely any would have been penned had people thought Jesus remained in the grave. It's doubtful Christianity itself would have emerged. It's hard to overestimate the importance of Jesus' resurrection for Christianity.

Writers of scripture believed God raised Jesus from the dead. The resurrection gave Jesus authority. Scripture writers believed Jesus continued living, and today most Christians think Jesus is alive in some sense. New Testament writers also thought Jesus' resurrection tells us about the afterlife possibilities for all humans and the fate of all creation.

There is no consensus on what *exactly* happened at Jesus' resurrection. The biblical accounts are far from clear. No eyewitnesses were present at the moment of resurrection. Among contemporary theories explaining what happened, four are prominent.

One theory says Jesus came out of the grave with a physical body almost exactly like the one placed in the tomb. A second says Jesus was transformed into a spiritual or glorified body with physical dimensions. A third says God raised Jesus as a spirit or soul, and post-resurrection witnesses encountered Jesus as a psycho-spiritual reality. A fourth theory says God raised Jesus only in the minds of believers.[1]

The first and fourth theories seem least likely. People who witnessed the risen Jesus describe him acting in ways not possible for a person with a normal body. He can walk through walls, stroll for miles or stand next to friends unrecognized, and appear instantaneously to individuals or groups. A radical transformation seems to have occurred; the risen body isn't identical to one placed in the tomb.

The fourth theory also seems unlikely. It rightly points to the inspiration Jesus' resurrection gives. But it cannot account well for eyewitness testimonies. When encountering the risen Jesus, people seemed to experience something beyond their imagination. The resurrection isn't "just in their heads."

Jesus, his followers, and many in the first century believed in life after death. Jesus' own words and stories are evidence of this, even if he failed to provide detail on what resurrections entail. The biblical accounts are hints about the afterlife rather than full descriptions. But they point to continued subjective experiences beyond bodily death.

The New Testament sometimes says resurrection involves becoming transformed into what the Apostle Paul called "spiritual bodies."[2] It's not clear if these bodies have physical dimensions. Perhaps they're like apparitions. Perhaps they're embodied souls. Perhaps they are spirits with both mental and physical dimensions. Perhaps...

I'm only skimming the surface of the diverse ideas biblical writers have about the afterlife. A full account of the afterlife possibilities requires at least a book. The Old and New

Testament views of the afterlife seem to be evolving. My main points are these: despite imprecision, Jesus and other biblical writers are confident the afterlife is real. And this afterlife seems to involve what many call "continued subjective experience."

THE LOGIC OF LOVE

Christian views of the afterlife continued developing after the Bible was written, and multiple views have emerged. Most appeal to biblical passages, authorities in the tradition, arguments, and other sources. I draw from these sources for my relentless love view, but I lean heavily upon what I call "the logic of love." By this, I mean we should keep love central as we think about what might occur after our bodies die.

Readers of *God Can't* know I think the themes of love are central to scripture. The overall drift of the Bible points to a loving God. This God calls humans to love. Jesus' life, teachings, death, and resurrection articulate these ideas too. He reveals a God who loves everyone and everything. We and others benefit when we cooperate with God's loving activity.

As I explained in an earlier chapter, to love is to act intentionally, in relational response to God and others, to promote overall well-being.[3] We love when we aim to help, do good, and promote flourishing. To love is to be a blessing in relation to God, others, and creation.

The Bible offers strong reasons to think God wants the well-being of all, not just some. Love for all is primary in God's nature, so God always loves others. God engages in giving and receiving love when creating, healing, promoting life, and generating wholeness. Love is so central to God that the Apostle John says, "God is love" (1 Jn 4:8, 16).

Despite God's loving activity, awful things happen. There's unnecessary suffering in the world. I won't lay out fully the uncontrolling love thesis again. But I'll simply say my view says God's love is inherently uncontrolling. Because God always loves everyone and everything, and because God's love can't control anyone or anything, God can't prevent evil singlehandedly.

My relentless love view of the afterlife assumes God loves everyone and everything. It assumes God's love is inherently uncontrolling. And it assumes God's love never ends: God never stops loving us and all creation. I call this the logic of God's uncontrolling love.

The logic of uncontrolling love grounds our hope for the afterlife.

AFTERLIFE AS HEAVEN AND HELL

Three theories pertaining to the afterlife prevail among Christians. The most common says after we die, God decides whether we go to Heaven or Hell. Our sins may influence God's decision. Whether we "accepted Jesus" or were faithful may influence it. How we treated the last and the least may affect what God decides. But after death, it's Heaven or Hell.

The Heaven and Hell theory says nothing we do *essentially* decides our fate. What happens is ultimately up to God. God has the power singlehandedly to send everyone to Heaven or everyone to Hell. The theory claims, however, God will decide some get eternal bliss, and others must endure eternal conscious torment.

The Heaven and Hell view implies God predetermined the criteria that decide our destiny. God set up the rules, decides whom to punish or reward, and executes judgment. The One who makes the rules could change them, because God is the sole lawmaker, judge, and implementer. But God is just, says this view, and some deserve everlasting torment.

The Heaven and Hell view has many critics, and I'm one of them. Most biblical scholars say the Bible does not support it. Never-ending conscious torment has little or no biblical basis. The theory's influence owes more to the medieval writer Dante than the Bible.

Several Hebrew and Greek words play central roles in why some believe in Hell. One word, as we've seen, is *Sheol*. Some biblical interpreters wrongly translate *Sheol* as "Hell," even though Old Testament writers did not believe *Sheol* involved punishment. Similarly, the New Testament word *Hades* has been wrongly translated "Hell." *Hades* comes from Greek religious-philosophical traditions, and it's the place good and bad people go after death. It's not a place of never-ending torment.

New Testament writers also use the word *Gehenna*, and scholars often translate it "Hell." It's the name of a valley outside Jerusalem. Children were sacrificed in fire at *Gehenna* long ago, and archeologists have evidence the valley was a burial ground. One Jewish tradition even suggests ancient people burned cadavers there. *Gehenna* was a place of death and destruction.

Jesus refers to *Gehenna* to describe the suffering and devastation that come from doing evil. Other New Testament writers refer to it as the negative consequences that come from sin. Most scholars consider *Gehenna* a metaphor to describe a life aimed at evil, not a fiery place where sinners go for never-ending punishment.

Jesus most criticizes those who don't help the hungry, naked, and imprisoned. Because the unrighteous fail to help "the least," he says, they endure "eternal fire" and "eternal punishment" (Mt. 25:31-45). Does this imply that Hell exists, and it involves everlasting conscious torment?

The New Testament word for "eternal" is *aionios*. But it's unclear whether *aionios* refers to an unending duration or intensity of experience. The debate is often framed in terms of quantity vs. quality. Do biblical references to "eternal punishment" mean unending quantity or intense quality of woe? The difference is important.

One argument against the unending quantity view builds from how the Apostle Paul uses *aionios*. In one passage, he says, "the revelation of the mystery was kept secret for long ages (*aionios*) but is now disclosed" (Rom. 16:25-26). Something "now disclosed" did not go on an unending quantity of time.[4] It wouldn't be "now" disclosed if it were endless. So "eternal" means something other than "unending duration."

Saying sin generates qualitatively negative experiences fits well with the broad biblical witness, contemporary health sciences, and our own experiences. Sin may be pleasurable in the short term, but it has long-term negative consequences. Sin may temporarily feel good for the sinner, but it eventually wreaks havoc on the sinner, others, and creation.

I earlier said I'm a critic of the Heaven and Hell view. This afterlife theory begins with the correct belief that actions have consequences. But it extends those consequences indefinitely into the afterlife — far beyond what is biblically or morally warranted. Infinite punishment doesn't fit the crime of finite sin.

The Heaven and Hell view cannot support the idea God *always* loves everyone. The God who sends some to never-ending torment isn't the forgiving God that Jesus reveals. This God isn't perfectly loving. For these and other reasons, the Heaven and Hell view of the afterlife fails to follow the logic of love. So I don't believe it.

UNIVERSALISM?

The second afterlife theory says God puts everyone in Heaven. Often called "universalism," this view says a *truly* loving God wouldn't condemn anyone to never-ending torment. No matter what we've done, God singlehandedly guarantees heavenly happiness for all.

Those who embrace universalism point to various biblical passages for support. "As in Adam all die, so also in Christ shall all be made alive," says Paul (1 Cor. 15:22). That sounds like everyone enjoys life everlasting. God will "reconcile all things to himself," Paul argues elsewhere (Col. 1:20). "No one is cast off by the Lord forever," says Lamentations, because God "will show compassion, so great is his unfailing love" (3:31-33). Advocates of universalism say these verses and others support their view that God saves everyone.

Perhaps the most persuasive biblical argument for universalism is general: a loving God forgives... always. "I blot out your transgressions," says God in the book of Isaiah, "and remember your sins no more" (43:25-26). Because "the Lord has forgiven us," says Paul, "so we ought to forgive others" (Col. 3:13). Our "sins are forgiven," says John, for the sake of God's name (1 Jn. 2:12). And so on.

Numerous ancient and contemporary Christians affirm universalism in some form.[5] The most common assumes God has the power to ensure Heaven for all. The sovereign God of the universe singlehandedly places all into Heaven, despite what they've done. Some say divine controlling is somehow compatible with creatures having freedom. Others say God initially created creatures in such a way they'd eventually choose Heaven. Let's call the idea a God capable of control will save everyone "common universalism."

I don't embrace the common universalism view. I like that it emphasizes God's love and forgiveness. I like that it says God sends no one to Hell. But I don't like what it assumes about God's power and creaturely freedom. The common view of universalism stands at odds with God's uncontrolling love and creaturely freedom. Let me explain.

First, the God with the controlling power necessary to put everyone in Heaven someday should use controlling power to stop evil right now. And yet evil occurs. A loving One who can control in the afterlife ought to prevent evil in *this* life.

Second, the common form of universalism ignores the freedom of those who *don't* want to be in Heaven. It says, "You have to be in Heaven, even if you don't want to." The Apostle Paul says love does not force its own way (1 Cor. 13:5), but this view disagrees.

Third, if we all end up enjoying everlasting bliss no matter what we do, our actions don't *ultimately* matter. Our choices don't *really* count if God singlehandedly rescues us. Our decisions are meaningless from an ultimate perspective.

Fourth, believing God sends everyone to eternal bliss undermines incentives to avoid evil, fight corruption, or combat climate change here and now.[6] Why endure the pain of self-sacrifice today if it doesn't matter for eternity? It's hard to care about the present if God sends everyone to bliss no matter what we do.

In sum, universalism has advantages over the Heaven and Hell view. But it also has problems. I aim to overcome those problems in my relentless love view of the afterlife.

ANNIHILATION?

The third afterlife scenario is the least known. It agrees that a loving God would send no one to never-ending torment. But it claims God destroys the unrepentant. God either annihilates them actively in a display of flashing omnipotence or passively by not sustaining their existence. God causes or allows the eradication of the unrighteous.

This view is often called "annihilationism" but sometimes "conditionalism." It takes literally rather than metaphorically biblical statements that say fire consumes the wicked (e.g., Heb. 6:8, 10:7). It takes as literal passages that talk of the wicked being destroyed (Mt. 7:13). Some build from the biblical claim God's love "is a consuming fire" and argue the unrepentant cannot be in the presence of divine love (Heb. 12:29).

In the annihilation view, God's active or passive destruction singlehandedly obliterates the unrepentant. Our afterlife existence is conditioned upon God's decision to keep us alive. Those exterminated get no second chances. If sinners wanted to repent at some later date, it's too late. God set up the rules, judges all, and follows through by eliminating the unrighteous.

I don't like the annihilation view. It rightly says our actions have consequences. It rightly says God sends no one to never-ending torment in Hell. But it assumes God quits. God gives up on some people. God does not forgive all but actively or passively destroys some. It implies divine love has limits.

I believe a God of everlasting love never gives up. God doesn't say, "I've given her 44,837 chances to repent, but no more!" Nor does God say, "I'd rather destroy him than forgive another time." I believe God *always* turns the other cheek — in this life and the next. The steadfast love of the Lord endures forever.

A God who annihilates is not a God of everlasting love and forgiveness.

RELENTLESS LOVE

The three afterlife theories we've explored say God alone decides our destiny. They assume God can decide our fate single-handedly. Consequently, each theory clashes with the logic of God's uncontrolling love.

The relentless love view starts from a different view of God's love and power. It builds from the belief that love is relational. God *needs* our cooperation for love to flourish. The relentless love view says we have genuine but limited freedom. But because of freedom, our choices truly matter.

At the heart of relentless love is the idea that God's love for all continues everlastingly, even beyond the grave. It builds from what the Psalmist calls the steadfast love of God. The writer of Lamentations puts it this way, "The steadfast love of the Lord never ceases; his mercies never come to an end" (Lam 3:22-23). The relentless love view takes as straightforwardly true what the Apostle Paul writes in his love chapter: "Love never gives up; it always hopes; it always endures" (1 Cor. 13:7).

The relentless love view assumes our hope now and later has God as its source. But it disagrees with theories that say God alone decides our fate. We also play a role. When we cooperate with divine love, we enjoy well-being. Goodness flourishes, and we experience abundant life. Cooperating with love brings the good life, healing, and flourishing.

When we do not cooperate with God, we suffer the natural negative consequences that come from failing to love. God doesn't punish. But there are natural negative consequences — in this life and the next — from saying no to positive and healthy choices. Sin is its own punishment.

The relentless love view extends the logic of uncontrolling love everlastingly. It rejects the idea God sends anyone to Hell. It rejects the idea God actively or passively annihilates. God does not put people in Heaven who don't want to be there. But God's love never quits. God's uncontrolling love makes possible continued subjective experiences — and choices — beyond our bodily death.

Good afterlife theories deal with the question of where we go after our bodily death. By "where," I mean the actual locations. Some say, "We go to be with God." But an omnipresent God is everywhere, so "being with God" occurs both now and after death. Others say we melt into the "mind of God." But if we keep a measure of individuality, the location question remains. I believe we should remain open to the possibility that afterlife bliss may occur near to or on earth, somewhere in our galaxy, or some other location.

Some religious traditions say those who do not cooperate with God endure time in purgatory, limbo, or purification. The relentless love view rejects these views... *if* they mean God punishes or creatures must earn divine favor. But if these words simply describe the process some people undergo on the way to realizing they should cooperate with God's love, these ideas are compatible with the relentless love view. Although God never controls and always invites to a love relationship, some may take longer to realize the wisdom in accepting this invitation to enjoy well-being.

THE GUARANTEES OF RELENTLESS LOVE

The relentless love view does not guarantee everyone will enjoy eternal bliss. But it provides the hope of universal salvation. An uncontrolling God cannot ensure that every creature will cooperate with love. But love is like that: it does not force its way (1 Cor. 13:5). The relentless love view has other guarantees, however. It guarantees love wins — in several ways.[7]

First, the God whose nature is uncontrolling love *never* stops loving us. Because love comes first in God's nature, God *cannot* stop loving. Many theologies say God may love us now, and God may love us after we die. But God could torture or destroy us. I can't imagine a loving person sending people to never-ending Hell or annihilating them. Love forgives. The God of relentless love, by contrast, *always* loves!

Love wins, because it's guaranteed God's relentless love works for well-being in the afterlife.

Second, the relentless love view says those who say "Yes" to God's love in the afterlife experience heavenly bliss. They enjoy abundant life in either a different (spiritual) body or as a bodiless soul. Those who cooperate and say "Yes!" to love are guaranteed life eternal. That's the good news of salvation.

Love wins, because it's guaranteed those who cooperate with God's relentless love will enjoy afterlife bliss.

Third, God *never* stops inviting us to love. Although some may not cooperate, God never throws in the towel. Natural negative consequences result from refusing love. But these consequences are self-imposed, not divinely inflicted. God doesn't punish and never stops calling us to embrace love.

Love wins, because it's guaranteed God always offers us the choice of love.

Fourth, the relentless love view says habits of love shape us into loving people. As we consistently say "Yes" to God, we develop loving characters. Those who develop loving characters through consistent positive responses grow less and less likely to choose unloving options. Developing a loving character may happen quickly or take more time. But we become radically new creations as we cooperate with love.

Love wins, because consistent cooperation with God's relentless love guarantees the development of loving characters.

Finally, we have good reason to *hope* all creatures eventually cooperate with God. It's reasonable to think the God who never gives up and whose love is universal will eventually convince all. Comprehensive cooperation is not guaranteed by divine fiat, because God's love is uncontrolling. But we have genuine hope all will eventually cooperate, because time is on the side of an everlasting God.

In sum, bliss beyond the grave rests primarily, but not exclusively, on the relentless love of God. How we respond to God's love matters now and later. The logic of uncontrolling love offers a new explanation of what happens to us after death. That logic leads to the relentless love view of the afterlife.

And in this view, love wins.

WILL EVERYONE COOPERATE?

The ultimate victory of good over evil requires creatures to cooperate with God. At times, this seems inevitable. I see good winning, and I'm optimistic about the future. At other times, it seems impossible. The world has so many problems, and some people rarely seem to cooperate with God. Sometimes people and systems seem hopelessly evil!

We can trust God to act for a good today and tomorrow. It's God's nature to love all creation, so God never gives up. But the relentless love view requires creatures to cooperate for all to be right. Is hope for comprehensive creaturely cooperation realistic? Is the idea all creation will be redeemed through cooperation with God a pipe dream, fantasy, or hopelessly naïve wish?

Theologian John Wesley wrestled with this question. As a thought experiment about creation's destiny, Wesley wrote, "Suppose the Almighty to act *irresistibly*." On this view, he says, "all difficulty that the world would be saved vanishes away." A controlling God could guarantee universal salvation.

But this thought experiment leads to an insurmountable problem. If God were to control us, says Wesley, "man would be man no longer; his inmost nature would be changed. He would no longer be a moral agent, any more than the sun or the wind, as he would no longer be endued with liberty, a power of choosing or self-determination. Consequently, he would no longer be capable of virtue or vice, of reward or punishment."[8]

Wesley's general view of salvation is, as he puts it, "God will not save us without ourselves." This means we play an essential role in our redemption and the redemption of all creation.[9] Although he does not use the language of God's relentless or uncontrolling love, his logic seems the same. I think Wesley would like my relentless love view!

But this leaves our question unanswered. Will all creation eventually cooperate with God's work of love? Could Wesley genuinely hope for the reconciliation of everyone and everything despite believing God would not save irresistibly?

Wesley was hopeful about the redemption of everyone and all creation. I find his logic of hope and love helpful. "In the same manner as God *has* converted so many to himself without destroying their liberty," he says, "God *can* undoubtedly convert whole natures or the whole world. It is as easy for him to convert a world as one individual soul."[10]

When I'm pessimistic all creatures will cooperate, I ponder Wesley's words. His optimism stems from God's relentless love. Then I ask myself, "Has God persuaded *me* to cooperate with love?"

I answer, "Yes!"

Then I ask, "If God can persuade me, why can't God persuade others? Am I better than them?"

I quickly answer my question: "No! I'm no better than others."

If God can persuade me, I have hope based on the evidence of my life (and the lives of others) that God will eventually persuade all creation. That's hope based primarily on God's relentless love!

WHAT HOPE DO WE HAVE IF GOD'S LOVE IS UNCONTROLLING?

Our hope rests ultimately on God's relentless yet uncontrolling love. This love grounds the possibility for positive change in the present and after we die. But we must cooperate with God's love for well-being to be established.

God does not send anyone to eternal conscious torment. But God doesn't force anyone into Heaven. God never annihilates through a flash of omnipotence or passive failure to resurrect. Instead, God calls and empowers all to respond in love in this life and the next. And divine love never gives up.

God's relentless but uncontrolling love grounds our hope now and for the future!

CHAPTER EIGHT

Do you _know_ God can't prevent evil singlehandedly?

Many readers of God Can't _or_ The Uncontrolling Love of God like the ideas I propose. But they wonder if I'm certain these ideas are correct. They ask, "How do you know you're right?" Or "Are you _sure_ about all of this?" Even, "Can you _prove_ it?"

I quickly respond to such questions by saying, "I'm not certain about these ideas." In fact, I don't think such certainty is possible for anyone. The most important ideas in life can't be deduced from unquestioned first principles or run through an irrefutable calculus.

But I'm not making up these ideas on the spot. I don't randomly throw proposals against a wall to see what sticks. This isn't rolling dice. Instead, I'm proposing a model — a theory about who God is, how God acts, and what the world is like — I think makes sense. The model draws from various resources, including the Bible, but not _just_ the Bible. It seeks truth wherever it can be found.

I don't even know with certainty God exists. So it would be foolish for me to say the model of God I propose is obviously correct. The uncontrolling love of God model is plausible, in fact, the most plausible model I know. But plausibility rests between blind faith and absolute certainty, between "I can't know anything" and "I'm 100% sure." Plausible models build from arguments and experiences, various sources, and the way the world seems to work.

MY JOURNEY

Questions about certainty play an important role in my life. I was fortunate to have been raised by parents and a faith community in which loving relationships were often modeled. No one and no group is perfect. But my upbringing was generally positive.

I left for college planning to pursue a degree in communications. Before long, I switched from communications to double major in psychology and social work. A few years later, I switched again and completed my undergraduate career with a degree in religion.

During my last year of college, I encountered arguments contrary to my views of God. They came from intelligent agnostics, atheists, and those from other religious traditions. I was studying history's smartest critics of Christianity, and I took their arguments seriously. In light of this research, my reasons for believing in God no longer made sense. So, I left the faith.

Prior to my studies, I'd been someone who took Christian beliefs seriously. I witnessed door-to-door, in bars and beaches, and on streets. I joined Campus Crusade for Christ, because I liked their aggressive evangelism style. I was compelled to share the "right" ideas about God. I was no "half-hearted," "lukewarm," or "wishy-washy" Christian.

I'm not the first person to leave faith in God and become an atheist or agnostic. People abandon belief in God for various reasons. Some are abused by religious people and consequently no longer want to associate with the faith of their abusers. Others give up faith as rebellion against family, friends, or culture. Some seem to reject faith to set aside the moral codes, the "dos and don'ts" they were taught. And others give up belief in God because, like me, the reasons they once embraced no longer make sense.

For the sake of intellectual honesty, I stopped believing in God.

I eventually re-believed. My return to faith occurred largely because I persisted in wrestling with the possibility of God's existence. I never gave up the intellectual quest. Two issues were central in my return.

My search for meaning was one reason I re-believed in God. I could not make ultimate sense of life if something like what most people called "God" did not exist. This search for meaning led me — and still leads me — to think it's plausible a God exists who grounds ultimate meaning.

Love was the second issue central to my return. Deep down, I sensed that I and others ought to love. I couldn't make sense of this intuition if there did not exist a being who was the ultimate source of love. It seemed plausible this being could be my guide for what love ought to look like. One might say *love* led me back to God.

Love remains central to how I understand God and think about existence. At its best, Christianity makes love central, so

I consider myself a Christian. I aim to follow Jesus' love, and I have a special affinity with others who try to do the same. I also find I share more in common with those who do not identify as Christian but love consistently than those who identify as Christian but don't love consistently.

To me, love matters more than religious identity.

CERTAINTY

Many who ask the question that shapes this chapter worry about being uncertain. I understand why some want a sure foundation upon which to place their most important beliefs. They want to be intellectually secure about what matters most.

I once thought questioning, doubt, and uncertainty were signs of immaturity. I thought anyone who was not positive God exists was a child in the faith. I was told doubting was sinful, and I sang, "Trust and obey." Certainty about God seemed the Christian's goal.

I no longer think mature people should be certain about God's existence. It's plausible to me God exists, and I have a reasonable faith or fundamental trust God is present and active in the world. I can point to arguments, evidence, personal and communal experiences, and more to support my beliefs. But I'm not sure about God's existence, in the sense of having no reasonable doubts.

I worry, in fact, when people say they're certain God exists. These same people act as if they know without question who God is, as if they've figured out the divine. I guess it would be strange to say you're certain God exists but not certain who God is! Kudos to them for consistency.

Brazen certainty leads almost inevitably to pride. Surety tempts us to ridicule, devalue, or destroy those who have a different view of God or no view at all. By contrast, I think doubt is fundamental to the good life. Doubt is an aspect of belief. Christians are "believers" not "certainers," to coin a word. I like what Phineas Bresee says on this: "Faith isn't the absence of doubt; it's choosing to act despite doubt."

Some see problems with certainty and take the opposite approach: blind faith. They think a genuine believer affirms God's existence having no evidence and no good arguments. "You just need to have faith," some say, by which they seem to mean setting aside reason and evidence altogether. Those who believe blindly easily become pawns for charlatans and swindlers.

I recommend a middle way. It steers a path between certainty God exists and blind faith. It's the "plausible" approach I mentioned earlier.[1] I think the plausibility way fits the general drift of scripture, and my favorite saints model it. This *via media* promotes humble conviction and cautious confidence.

QUESTIONING

Because I frequently give lectures, I spend significant time on university campuses. I meet students who, to various degrees and in various ways, ask important questions. Most arrived at university expecting to be educated. This not only means adding knowledge, it also means setting aside some beliefs they once held dear. It's important to question, doubt, and wrestle with the biggest questions of life, and this often means setting aside previously persuasive answers to those questions.

Jennifer is a college chemistry professor and friend of mine. She likes to greet her first-year students and say, "Everything you learned in high school chemistry is wrong." Most students shrug and react positively. They entered college open to the possibility they might need to rethink some of what they previously understood about chemistry.

Several years ago, Jennifer dared me to begin my first-year religion classes with, "Everything you learned about God in Sunday school is wrong." I'm wise enough not to have accepted that dare! Not everything students learn in high school chemistry is wrong, of course, and neither is everything they learn in Sunday school. But part of the educational process involves reconceptualizing our previous views in the effort to find better ones.

According to statistics I've seen, most students don't give up faith in God. But most decide some of their previous ideas aren't worth keeping. Some of what they'd been taught by parents, grandparents, Sunday school teachers, or pastors no longer makes sense. They'll deconstruct ideas on a journey that leads to reconstructing new ones.

We must make space for everyone — especially university students — to do this reconceptualizing work. It can be heart wrenching for them... and for us. But if we respect the first of Jesus' commandments, which includes loving God with our minds, we must allow for changes of mind in others and ourselves.

If we want to love, we must allow space for questions and uncertainty.

UNCERTAINTY AND MYSTERY

Some who ask the question that shapes this chapter hear me say I'm not being certain God can't control others. They respond with an excellent follow-up: "What's the difference between saying you're not certain God is uncontrolling and saying, 'It's all a mystery?'"

As I've mentioned in previous chapters and books, I'm dissatisfied with those who play the mystery card in discussions of God and evil. Professional scholars and the average person on the street reach for the mystery card when argued into a corner. These believers are unwilling to give up the idea God can control, is loving, or that evil occurs. So out comes the mystery card in response to perhaps the most important question believers and unbelievers ask. "God's ways are not our ways," they say. "God's will is inscrutable." "God is hidden, so we must live with this question mark."

I don't play this mystery card. I don't appeal to divine hiddenness or the inscrutable divine will. I admit to having limited knowledge and, as the Apostle Paul put it, looking through a darkened glass (1 Cor. 13:12). But to admit to having limited knowledge differs from the appeal to mystery so many make.

Those who want to give an account of the hope they have in God should offer a model of God — a theology — without gaping holes on the questions that matter most. We ought to judge the models of God offered, even though we can't know with certainty which is closest to being fully true. If some models have gaping holes, we should consider them less adequate than those without holes.

Let me illustrate this. Suppose while hiking through Idaho, I find a soda bottle with a message inside. The message indicates the bottle came from someone in Nairobi, Kenya. I would naturally wonder how this bottle and message traveled halfway around the globe to North America.

Suppose we gathered five people unaware of the bottle's actual journey. We asked each to speculate how it traveled from Kenya to Idaho. And suppose we also assemble a panel of judges to read the speculations of these five people and assess which seemed most plausible.

The five submitted their speculative explanations, and the judges read each. One person guessed that the bottle traveled north out of Africa through Israel and eventually to the shores of France. Another speculated the bottle traversed north and east through the Asian continent to China's eastern ocean shores. Others offered their own guesses on how the bottle left Nairobi and traveled to an ocean. The speculations also differed on how the bottle traveled to Idaho once it reached North America. Each theory had a measure of plausibility.

Let's suppose, however, the judges found something surprising. Only one of the five explanations offered an account of how the bottle traversed the oceans. Four offered no possible explanation for how the bottle traveled this crucial leg of the trek from Kenya to Idaho. Not accounting for how the bottle passed across the waters separating continents seriously undermines the overall plausibility of four explanations! The one explanation that offered a full account may not be correct. But it's more plausible than the four alternatives.

Let me apply this bottle illustration to questions of mystery and uncertainty. Most Christians I know say God allows evil. They think permitting evil is mysteriously consistent with God's perfect love. The greatest and not-so-great theologians argue this way, because they presuppose God could prevent evil singlehandedly.

Failing to provide a plausible answer for why a loving God doesn't prevent genuine evil is like explaining how a bottle traveled from Kenya to Idaho without accounting for how it crossed an ocean. A theology that fails to account for evil is like a traveling bottle explanation that fails to account for oceans.[2]

IS PROGRESS POSSIBLE?

I began this book with a sampling of the many letters I've received since writing *God Can't*. I'm happy the book's ideas are helping people!

Given this positive response, I naturally wonder whether the *God Can't* ideas might help even more people. I wonder who else might find the uncontrolling love view persuasive, and what other questions might this view of God answer. This book intends to show that the uncontrolling love view can answer other vexing questions while accounting for the positive aspects in conventional views of God.

But can these ideas gain traction to make a bigger difference? Answering this question requires answering a larger one: is *any* progress possible?

The idea life could get better strikes some as naïve. These people point to pandemics, wars, ecological disasters, political elections, racial injustice, and more that's wrong in the world. To them, it's absurd to think things could get better. The world seems to get worse, from this perspective. Let's call these people "pessimists."

Pessimists admit progress of a certain sort can be made. Humans might produce more commodities, for instance. Computer complexity is increasing and seems likely to continue for the foreseeable future. Other technologies seem to advance, and we have access to more information than ever.

But pessimists say (and I think rightly) increases in commodities, computers, technology, or information don't indicate genuine progress. What we need is an increase in our quality of life. Often, commodities we thought would make life better make it worse. What we really want is a proliferation of well-being. *That* would be authentic progress.

Other people believe progress is inevitable. Let's call them the "optimists." Some in this camp are atheists who think overcoming religion with science is the path to progress. Others are believers who think God will control creation to guarantee a better future step by step. The "progress is inevitable" optimists point to reductions in diseases, increases in species complexity, greater overall human health, fewer large-scale wars, and more.

Admittedly, the number of optimists — whether atheist or theist — has decreased as we've become more aware of the ecological crisis damaging our planet now and likely into the future. It's hard to be optimists when the plane and many of its life forms are in imminent danger or actual demise.

I find a third option — between pessimists and optimists — most compelling. This option says progress is *possible* but *not inevitable*. In terms of moral progress, this means love can make progress. Love can win. But we can also fail to love and witness the increase of evil. Love may lose.

Believing we can make moral progress as individuals, communities, and even cultures can protect us from despair. If progress was impossible, hopelessness would be appropriate. If progress was inevitable, what we do would not matter.

If the third option is correct — progress is possible but not inevitable — what we do matters and a better future can be established.[3]

To say progress is possible but not inevitable fits well the *God Can't* view that God is uncontrolling. This God of love always acts and influences, so we have reason to hope for something better. Our hope is grounded in the uncontrolling God who invites us and all creation to love in response. When we cooperate, progress occurs. If we respond poorly, destruction and ruin take place. The future is open, and how we act makes a difference in what will become reality.[4]

Applying all of this to my question about the future of the uncontrolling love perspective, I conclude it *may* have a wider influence and make a bigger difference. *If* these ideas describe who God is and how God acts, we might even say God *wants* the *God Can't* ideas to spread. I can't know this with certainty, of course, but it seems plausible.

Sharing the uncontrolling love ideas requires action. We all have a role to play, but each role will be unique. It's not all about me, and I can only do a tiny part. You can do a part too. Together, our tiny parts can make a real difference.

DO YOU *KNOW* GOD CAN'T PREVENT EVIL SINGLEHANDEDLY?

I don't know with certainty the ideas of the uncontrolling love view are correct. I think it's plausible the view is true, however. These ideas fit how I read the Bible, the best of my intellectual abilities, and the way the world seems to work. Given the widest array of information and experiences, it makes sense to say a loving God can't prevent evil singlehandedly.

This book answers the primary questions *God Can't* readers ask. I hope it contributes to the progress we would all like to see. In writing it, I don't believe I'm smarter, wiser, or cleverer than everyone. I'm also not interested in self-promotion; the ideas and their impact interest me. And I don't expect everyone who endorses the uncontrolling love of God perspective to agree with what I've proposed in this book.[5] Smart and good people can have differing opinions.

I wrote this book because these ideas have helped me. And they're helping others. They seem part of the mix of what can improve our lives. And helping us all — promoting overall well-being — is the point of love.

Will the uncontrolling love of God ideas spread? I hope so. The future depends upon God, us, and others. You and I play an essential part. This book is my attempt to spread the good news of a God who loves everyone in an uncontrolling way. I encourage you to consider what you might do.

Progress in love is possible.

Endnotes

Preface

1. Thomas Jay Oord, *God Can't! How to Believe in God and Love after Tragedy, Abuse, and Other Evils* (Grasmere, Id.: SacraSage, 2019); Spanish Translation: *Dios No Puede: Como Creer en Dios y el Amor Despues de la Tragedia, el Abuso y Otros Males,* Lemuel Sandoval, trans. (SacraSage, 2019); German Translation: *GOTT kann das nicht! Wie man trotz Tragödien, Missbrauch oder anderem Unheil den Glauben an Gott und Seine Liebe bewahrt,* Michael Trenkel and Dirk Weisensee, trans. (SacraSage, 2019).

Introduction: *God Can't* is Helping People

1. For chapter-length stories from those who have been helped by the uncontrolling love view, see L Michaels, ed. *What about Us? Stories of Uncontrolling Love* (Grasmere, Id.: SacraSage, 2019).

2. See *The Uncontrolling Love of God* (Downers Grove, Ill.: IVP Academic, 2015), ch. 7.

3. See Jürgen Moltmann, "God's Kenosis in the Creation and Consummation of the World," in *The Work of Love: Creation as Kenosis,* ed. John C. Polkinghorne (Grand Rapids: Eerdmans, 2001), 146.

4. Bradford McCall explores this idea in relation to emergence, *A Modern Relation of Theology and Science Assisted by Kenosis and Emergence* (Wipf and Stock, 2018).

5. On this, see my essay "Genuine (but Limited) Freedom for Creatures and for a God of Love" In *Neuroscience and Free Will,* James Walters and Philip Clayton, eds. (Eugene, Or.: Pickwick, 2020).

6. Lisa Michaels, et. al., eds. *Uncontrolling Love: Essays Exploring the Love of God, with Introductions by Thomas Jay Oord* (San Diego, CA: SacraSage, 2017).

1. If God can't control, why pray?

1. Christopher Fisher defends the open view that supports this claim by exploring various biblical passages. See his *God is Open: Examining the Open Theism of the Biblical Authors* (CreateSpace, 2017).

2. Greg Boyd has used the idea of Satan and demons when formulating his open and relational theology. Among his many books on the subject, see *Satan and the Problem of Evil: Constructing a Trinitarian Warfare Theodicy* (Downers Grove, IL: InterVarsity Press, 2001);

3. For outstanding books on prayer among the many available, see Mark Karris, *Divine Echoes: Reconciling Prayer with the Uncontrolling Love of God* (Orange, California: Quior, 2018); Marjorie Suchocki, *In God's Presence: Theological Reflections on Prayer* (St. Louis, Mo.: Chalice, 1996); Bruce Epperly, *Praying with Process Theology: Spiritual Practices for Personal and Planetary Healing* (River Lane, 2017).

4. Philip Clayton lays out some of these implications in *Transforming Christian Theology: For Church and Society* (Philadelphia: Fortress, 2009).

2. If God is uncontrolling, how do we explain miracles?

1. David Hume, "An Enquiry Concerning Human Understanding," in *On Human Nature and the Understanding*, ed. Antony Flew (1748; repr., New York: Collier, 1962), 119.

2. Alfred North Whitehead offers a stringent criticism of Hume in his magnum opus, *Process and Reality: An Essay in Cosmology*, ed. David Ray Griffin and Donald W. Sherburne, corrected ed. (1929; New York: Free, 1978).

3. See *The Uncontrolling Love of God*, ch. 2.

4. I explain the issues of love and inanimate/aggregate objects in my essay, "Love, Society, and Machines," in *Love, Technology, and Theology*, Scott A. Midson, ed. (London: T&T Clark, 2020.)

5. John Sanders has wondered whether my uncontrolling love view accounts for miracles. Richard Rice joins Sanders's wondering in *The Future of Open Theism: From Antecedents to Opportunities* (Downers Grove, Ill.: IVP Academic, 2020). I show in the present book how my view accounts for miracles and therefore answer Sanders and Rice. See also my response to Sanders in "Miracles, Theodicy, and Essential Kenosis: Response to Sanders," *Wesleyan Theological Journal*. 53:2 (2018): 194-215.

6. For helpful references on miracles, see Craig S. Keener's work *Miracles: The Credibility of the New Testament Accounts*, 2 vols. (Grand Rapids: Baker Books, 2011) and Paul Alexander, *Signs and Wonders: Why Pentecostalism Is the World's Fastest Growing Faith* (San Francisco: Jossey-Bass, 2009).

7. See *The Uncontrolling Love of God*, ch. 8.

8. For a general discussion of biblical reasons for denying that God controls, see Terence E. Fretheim, *About the Bible: Short Answers to Big Questions*, rev. ed. (Minneapolis: Augsburg, 2009), pp. 93-98. 14. For a Pentecostal-Charismatic argument similar to my own, see Joshua D. Reichard, "Of Miracles and Metaphysics: A Pentecostal-Charismatic and Process-Relational Dialog," Zygon: Journal of Religion and Science 48 (2013): 274-93. See also Amos Yong, in *The Spirit of Creation: Modern Science and Divine Action in the Pentecostal-Charismatic Imagination* (Grand Rapids: Eerdmans, 2011), ch. 4.

9. Terrence Fretheim, *Exodus: Interpretation* (Philadelphia: Westminster John Knox, 2004), 97, 99.

10. Brevard Childs, another eminent Old Testament scholar, argues like I do in his commentary, *The Book of Exodus: A Critical, Theological Commentary* (Louisville, KY: Westminster John Knox, 2004), 174).

11. For more on my views of panpsychism and material-mental monism, see "Panentheism and Panexperientialism for Open and Relational Theology," with Andrew Schwartz, in *Panentheism and Panpsychism*, in *Panentheism and Panpsychism: Philosophy of*

Religion Meets Philosophy of Mind, Godehard Brüntrup, Benedikt Paul Göcke, and Ludwig Jaskolla, eds. (Mentis Verlag/Brill, 2020).

12. One of the best philosophical arguments for panpsychism in relation to the mind-body problem is David Ray Griffin, *Unsnarling the World-Knot: Consciousness, Freedom, and the Mind-Body Problem* (University of California Press, 1998).

3. What does an uncontrolling God do?

1. Keith Ward is one of the most persuasive and productive advocates of God as a mind or soul of the universe. Among his many books, see *The Christian Idea of God* (Cambridge University Press, 2017).

2. See, for instance, my essay, "The Divine Spirit as Causal and Personal," *Zygon*. 48:2 (June 2013): 454-465.

3. Bishop Robert Barron, "Bishop Barron Governor Cuomo and the Nature of God https://www.youtube.com/watch?v=Igl29K3DC8w (accessed 5/18/20)

4. One of the clearest scholarly advocates for the view I'm rejecting comes from Michael Dodds. See my review of his book, *Unlocking Divine Action: Contemporary Science and Thomas Aquinas* in *Christian Scholar's Review* 43, no. 2 (Winter 2013).

5. See Anna Case-Winters arguments in *God's Power: Traditional Understandings and Contemporary Challenges* (Louisville, KY: Westminster John Knox, 1990).

6. Arthur Holmes, "Why God Cannot Act," in *Process Theology*, Ronald Nash, ed. (Grand Rapids, Mich.: Baker, 1987).

7. William Lane Craig, "Responses" in *God and the Problem of Evil: Five Views*. James K. Dew, Jr. and Chad Meister, eds. (Downers Grove, Ill.: InterVarsity Press, 2017).

4. What does it mean to say God loves everyone and everything?

1. See *Defining Love: A Philosophical, Scientific, and Theological Engagement* (Grand Rapids, Mich.: Brazos, 2010); *The Nature of Love: A Theology* (St. Louis, Mo.: Chalice, 2010); *The Science of Love: Wisdom of Well-Being* (Philadelphia: Templeton, 2005).

2. Brian McLaren writes eloquently about this love in chapter three of *The Great Spiritual Migration* (Hodder and Staughton, 2016).

3. My view fits the views of a large number of Old Testament scholars. On the question of God's violence, see especially Eric Seibert, *The Violence of Scripture: Overcoming the Old Testament's Troubling Legacy* (Philadelphia: Fortress, 2012).

4. For a book of introductory essays on relational theology, see Brint Montgomery, Karen Winslow, and Thomas Jay Oord, eds. *Relational Theology: A Contemporary Introduction* (San Diego: Point Loma University Press, 2012).

5. Thomas Aquinas, *Summa Theologica*, I (Westminster, Md.: Christian Classics, 1981), q. 6, a.2, ad 1.

6. Thomas Aquinas, *Summa Contra Gentiles* II (Notre Dame, Ind.: University of Notre Dame Press, 1981), 13-14.

7. St. Anselm, *Proslogium*, tr. Sidney Norton Deane (La Salle, IL, 1951), pp. 13-14.

8. The literature on God and the open future is immense and persuasive. Among the important works, see Clark Pinnock et al., *The Openness of God: A Biblical Challenge to the Traditional Understanding of God* (Downers Grove, IL: InterVarsity Press, 1994); John Sanders *The God Who Risks: A Theology of Providence*, rev. ed. (Downers Grove, IL: InterVarsity Press, 2007).

9. I explain the essential relatedness of God in "Strong Passibility," and "My Response," in *Four Views of Divine Impassibility*, Robert Matz, ed. (Downers Grove, Ill.: Intervarsity, 2019).

10. Kevin's essay is "Love without Measure: John Webster's Unfinished Dogmatic Account of the Love of God in Conversation with Thomas Jay Oord's Interdisciplinary Account." My full-length response is "Analogies of Love between God and Creatures: Thomas Jay Oord Responds to Kevin Vanhoozer." Find these essays in *Love, Human and Divine: Contemporary Essays in Systematic and Philosophical Theology* Oliver D. Crisp, James M. Arcadi, Jordan Wessling, eds. (T & T Clark Publishers, 2019).

5. How does Jesus fit in a theology of uncontrolling love?

1. For a similar approach, see Tripp Fuller, *The Homebrewed Christianity Guide to Jesus: Liar, Lunatic, Lord, or Awesome?* (Philadelphia: Fortress, 2015).

2. In addition to Moltmann's essay cited in footnote 2 above, see these ideas in *God in Creation* (London: SCM Press, 1985), 87.

3. See Roger E. Olson, "What's Wrong with Calvinism?," My Evangelical Arminian Theological Musings (blog), Evangelical Channel, Patheos, March 22, 2013, www.patheos.com/blogs/rogereolson/2013/03/whats-wrong-with-calvinism.

4. John C. Polkinghorne, "Kenotic Creation and Divine Action," in *The Work of Love: Creation as Kenosis*, ed. John C. Polkinghorne (Grand Rapids: Eerdmans, 2001), 102. I generally find Polkinghorne's thought helpful. For an overview, see *The Polkinghorne Reader* (London: SPCK Press; Philadelphia: Templeton Foundation Press, 2010).

6. If God created the universe, why can't God stop evil?

1. For the problems that come from accepting creation from nothing as they relate to climate change, see my essay "God's Initial and Ongoing Creation, "in *Christian theology and Climate Change*. Hilda P. Koster and Ernst M Conradie, eds. (London: T&T Clark, 2019).

2. Claus Westermann, *Genesis 1-11. A Commentary*, John J. Scullion, S. J., trans. (London: SPCK, 1994), 110.

3. Terence E. Fretheim, *God and World in the Old Testament: A Relational Theology of Creation* (Nashville: Abingdon, 2005), 5.

4. Jon D. Levenson, *Creation and the Persistence of Evil: The Jewish Drama of Divine Omnipotence* (Princeton, N.J.: Princeton University Press, 1994; New York: Harper & Row, 1987), 121.

5. Mark S. Smith, *The Priestly Vision of Genesis 1* (Philadelphia: Fortress, 2010), 50.

6. Rolf P. Knierim, *Task of Old Testament Theology* (Grand Rapids, Mich.: Eerdmans, 1995), 210.

7. See also Bruce K. Waltke, *Creation and Chaos* (Portland, OR: Western Conservative Baptist Seminary, 1974); Shalom M. Paul, "Creation and Cosmogony: In the Bible," *Encyclopedia Judaica* (Jerusalem: Keter, 1972), 5:1059-63; Frances Young, "Creatio Ex Nihilo:

A Context for the Emergence of Christian Doctrine of Creation," *Scottish Journal of Theology* 44 (1991): 139-51; Keith Norman, *"Ex Nihilo*: The Development of the Doctrines of God and Creation in Early Christianity," *BYU Studies* 17/3 (1977): 291-318. John H. Walton, *The Lost World of Genesis One: Ancient Cosmology and the Origins Debate* (Downers Grove, IL: IVP, 2009), 42.

8. Gerhard May, *Creatio Ex Nihilo: The Doctrine of 'Creation out of Nothing' in Early Thought* Trans. A. S. Worrall (Edinburgh: T & T Clark, 1994), 74.

9. Michael Lodahl explores love as God's motive for creating in *God of Nature and of Grace: Reading the World in Wesleyan Ways* (Nashville: Abingdon, 2004).

10. I'm grateful to David Ray Griffin for first introducing me to the possibility God created prior to our universe. For his view on this possibility, see David Ray Griffin, *Reenchantment without Supernaturalism: A Process Philosophy of Religion* (Ithaca, NY: Cornell University Press, 2001), 137-143.

11. I lay out these ideas in "God Always Creates Out of Creation in Love," in *Theology of Creation: Creatio ex Nihilo and Its New Rivals*, Thomas Jay Oord, ed. New York: Routledge, 2014.

12. Panentheism is defined in various ways. See Philip Clayton and Arthur Peacocke, eds. *In Whom We Live and Move and Have our Being: Panentheistic Reflections on God's Presence in a Scientific World* (Grand Rapids, Mich.: Eerdmans, 2004); Andrew Davis and Philip Clayton, eds. *How I Found God in Everyone and Everything* (Monkfish, 2018); Benedikt Göcke, "Panentheism and Classical Theism," *Sophia*, 52 (2013): 61-75; Ryan Mullins, "The Difficulty with Demarcating Panentheism," *Sophia*, 55 (2016): 325–346.

7. What hope do we have if God's love is uncontrolling?

1. Find one of the better overviews of the resurrection possibilities in John Hick, *Death and Eternal Life* (Philadelphia: Westminster John Knox, 1994).

2. I Cor. 15:42-44.

3. I explain my definition in detail in several books. See especially *Defining Love* and *The Nature of Love*.

4. A classic work on the meaning of *aion* and *aionios* is John Wesley Hanson, *The Greek Word Aion-Aionios Translated Everlasting Eternal in the Holy Bible Shown to Denote Limited Duration* (Chicago: Northwestern Universalist Publishing House, 1875). Find it online at 0000000000000000

5. For an accessible defense of universalism, see Keith Giles, *Jesus Undefeated: Condemning the False Doctrine of Eternal Torment* (Quior, 2019). For a much less accessible case for universalism, see David Bentley Hart, *That All Shall Be Saved: Heaven, Hell, and Universal Salvation* (Yale University Press, 2019). For a strong biblical appraisal of universalism, see Bradley Jersak, *Her Gates Will Never Be Shut: Hell, Hope, and the New Jerusalem* (Wipf and Stock, 2005).

6. Among the many organizations working against climate change for a new way to live as a civilization, see the Institute for Ecological Civilization. For explanations of what an "ecological civilization" looks like, see Philip Clayton and Wm Andrew Schwartz, *What is Ecological Civilization?* (Process Century, 2019) and Jay McDaniel and Patricia Adams Farmer, *Replanting Ourselves in Beauty* (Process Century, 2015).

7. On the theme of love winning at the end, see Rob Bell, *Love Wins: A Book about Heaven, Hell, and the Fate of Every Person Who Ever Lived* (HarperCollins, 2011). For arguments against the typical view of Hell, see Sharon L. Baker Putt, *Razing Hell* (Westminster John Knox, 2010).

8. John Wesley, 'The General Spread of the Gospel', *The Works of John Wesley* (Kansas City: Nazarene Publishing House, 1872 authorized editor of the Wesleyan Conference Office), 6:280.

9. Ibid., 6:281.

10. Ibid.

8. Do you *know* God can't prevent evil singlehandedly?

1. Catherine Keller argues similarly in *On the Mystery: Discerning God in Process* (Minneapolis: Fortress, 2008).

2. I use this bottle illustration in "An Essential Kenosis Solution to the Problem of Evil," and "Response to Others" in *God and the Problem of Evil: Five Views*, James K. Dew, Jr. and Chad Meister, eds. (Downers Grove, Ill.: InterVarsity Press, 2017).

3. I lay out a civilization approach to this in "A Loving Civilization: A Political Ecology that Promotes Overall Well-Being," Evan Rosa, ed. (forthcoming).

4. Curtis Holtzen lays out what an open future means for God in his book *The God Who Trusts: A Relational Theology of Divine Faith, Hope, and Love* (Downers Grove, Ill.: Intervarsity Academic, 2019).

5. I see my work in this book as similar to what John Cobb did to explain possible implications for process when he wrote *The Process Perspective: Frequently Asked Questions About Process Theology*, Jeanyne B. Slettom, ed. (St. Louis: Chalice, 2003).

Acknowledgements

Many people helped me with this book. Some sent questions to consider, others read drafts and suggested edits. Some gave advice for the book's overall direction or provided insights for particular passages.

I am deeply grateful to Deborah Allenbaugh, Jordan Apodaca, Kathy Armistead, Kristina Armstrong, Justin Barksdale, Jane Bateman, Jez Bayes, Braidon Beard, Joshua Berwald, John Bosworth, Heather Borton, Alan Bradley, Michael Brennan, Tyler Brinkman, Josh Burton, Michelle Caldwell, Steve Carroll, Alex Chamberlain, Miriam Chickering, Michael Christensen, Terry Clees, John Cobb, Luke Taylor Cochran, Gloria Coffin, Tamara Coleman, Dave Coles, Emiko Cothran, John Dally, Lonnie Delisle, Brian Desmarais, Rob Duncan, William Eckert, Buford Edwards, Mike Edwards, Todd Erickson, Taryn Eudaly, Brian Felushko, Forest Fisk, Chris Fisher, Karl Forehand, Philip Fox, Simon Hall, Ryan Harbridge, Brittney Hartley, Christopher Heasty, Kristi Helbig, Chris Hill, Greg Hoover, JR Hustwit, Mark Karris, Damian

Kendrick, John Knight, Dan Koch, Mike Koolen, Cathy Lawton, Michael Lodahl, Bob Luhn, Ian Markham, Justin McClain, Robina McCron, Jay McDaniel, Shannon Mimbs, Brint Montgomery, Craig Morton, Hilde Marie Øgreid Movafagh, Heather Oglevie, Corey Ostler, Brett Parris, Nathan Patterson, Daniel Paul, Martinus Pretorius, Robin Rader, Michael Rans, Kat Rose, Shane Russo, Lemuel Sandoval, Andrew Schwartz, Andrew Sies, Russ Slater, Michele Oney Snyder, Fran Stedman, Dave Strauss, JP Tammen, Jaclyn Tarrant, Dan Taylor, Vernon Thillet, Ian Todd, Michael Turner, Jon Turney, Donna Ward, Adam Watkins, Chuck Wilkes, Jeff Williams.

Some of my best insights for this book came from social media discussions. I thank members of the following Facebook groups: Can I Say That in Church?, God is Open, Healing with God Can't, Homebrewed Christianity, Love Heretic, Misfits Theology Club, Open Horizons, Open and Relational, Open Theism, Process and Faith, The Reluctant Theologian, The Uncontrolling Love of God Conversations, and You Have Permission.

I also want to thank the institutions, groups, churches, seminaries, graduate schools, centers, and others who hosted me for lectures on topics I address in this book. I enjoy the interaction that comes from a live speaking experience. If your organization would like to invite me, find info on how to do so at my website: thomasjayoord.com

For more resources on open and relational theology, see the Center for Open and Relational Theology website: c4ort.com. And consider signing up for the center's monthly newsletters.

Index

Index

Like What You've Read?

Try these...

OPEN AND RELATIONAL LEADERSHIP

Leading with Love

Roland Hearn, Sheri D. Kling, & Thomas Jay Oord, EDITORS

THOMAS JAY OORD

The Uncontrolling Love *of* God

AN OPEN AND RELATIONAL ACCOUNT OF PROVIDENCE

What About Us?

STORIES OF UNCONTROLLING *Love*

L. MICHAELS

Uncontrolling *Love*

Essays Exploring the Love of God with Introductions by Thomas Jay Oord

Chris Baker, Gloria Coffin, Craig Drurey, Graden Kirksey, Lisa Michaels, Donna Fiser Ward

Made in the USA
Middletown, DE
07 September 2020

18922529R00120